MANPOWER PLANNING
FOR
HIGH TALENT PERSONNEL

MANPOWER PLANNING
FOR
HIGH TALENT PERSONNEL

ERIC W. VETTER
ASSISTANT PROFESSOR OF MANAGEMENT
Tulane University

BUREAU OF INDUSTRIAL RELATIONS
Graduate School of Business Administration
The University of Michigan
Ann Arbor

Printed in the United States of America

PREFACE

Planning for future manpower needs is now an ongoing activity in many organizations and institutions in the United States. Although a great deal has been written about the importance of manpower planning, much less has been written of what such planning involves or how to engage in it. The objective of this book is to provide information on the nature of manpower planning and to stimulate further thought upon, and investigation of, manpower planning problems.

A planning approach to manpower utilization can result in more effective management of the manpower resources of an organization. Through planning we are able to organize our manpower management efforts more systematically and to achieve important manpower goals. Such planning should embrace all aspects of manpower management in an organization. Successful treatment of all the manpower problems and questions in organizations, however, is not possible in any single book. Further, although many of the manpower problems we face today are of a long-standing nature, we have yet to arrive at satisfactory solutions to them. For example, how are a manager's leadership qualities to be effectively developed? Another unanswered problem is how to show, in economic terms, the value of a well-motivated group of workers.

Rather than attempt to cope with the multiplicity of manpower problems, the focus of this book is on analytical approaches that can be used to study the manpower situation in a specific organization — information of general applicability that is useful both to large and small organizations. Secondary treatment is given to means by which organizations meet their manpower problems. Solutions to these problems must be tailored to the characteristics and circumstances of the individual organizations.

This approach does not mean that every analytical tool for examining manpower is presented. Since the book is written for the person who lacks training in economics and statistics, some analytical tools of potential value are not presented. Those include statistical regression and correlation analysis, capital budgeting, economic model building, and Markovian processes for the study of manpower flow problems. The emphasis on analysis has, as a consequence, a lesser emphasis on many behavioral problems in manpower planning. These problems, such as resistance to change, are significant and influence the success of the manpower planning program.

Space considerations have placed limitations upon the book. This has meant that the discussion is narrowed to that portion of the workforce generally considered managerial in nature, including the "high talent" individuals generally assigned to the salaried-exempt payroll classification. Thus engineering, professional, and sales personnel are included in the expanded definition of managerial personnel. The exclusion of hourly and clerical workers from the discussion of planning obviously should not be interpreted to mean that planning should not be considered for them.

Space considerations have also dictated that some important or unusually difficult manpower problems are not given attention. These include the management of scientists and engineers, the staffing of international business ventures, the impact of manpower planning on society, the forecasting of specialized manpower skills, the impact of government legislation (e.g., equal opportunity regulations) on the firm, and manpower problems in mergers and acquisitions.

What are discussed, then, are some of the broader, more general aspects of manpower management. The material presented is organized in a somewhat unorthodox manner. Chapters 1 and 2 set the stage for the remainder of the book by developing the nature, need, and process of manpower planning. In Chapter 2 a schematic overview of the entire process is presented (Figure 2-1).

Attention then shifts to some of the end results of manpower planning in Chapter 3. These are programs which help the organization meet difficult manpower situations. The information presented has been gathered from interviews with manpower managers in a large number of organizations. The chapter does not review the literature available on the topics because of the magnitude of such a task.

Chapter 4 involves an analysis of inventory and forecast data to identify potential manpower problems. In Chapters 5 and 6, a discussion of how to measure labor productivity and to use the information in manpower forecasting is presented. This is an analytical discussion that hopefully is uncomplicated and meaningful to manpower managers. The area of manpower forecasting is still in early development and will require additional attention by other writers. Chapter 7 involves a presentation of how the manpower forecast can be related to other economic forecasts of the business organization. In Chapter 8 some fundamental ideas of control and evaluation and some indications of the role of control in manpower planning are presented. Chapter 9 takes up the question of the role of the manpower planner in the organization. Some of the important behavioral problems of manpower planning activities are suggested in this chapter to highlight potential barriers to a manpower planning program. Chapter appendixes are used to present special information that would otherwise interrupt the flow of ideas presented in the chapters.

This sequencing does not follow the manpower planning process sequence outlined in Chapter 2. Manpower forecasting logically precedes the design of action programs and the analysis of the management manpower structure. It is felt, however, that the arrangement used better demonstrates the need for the more involved methodological discussions in Chapters 5, 6, and 7.

Throughout the writing of the book an audience problem existed. Should the attention be directed toward the large corporation with an ongoing manpower planning program and sophisticated manpower management techniques, or should the concern be for the organization just beginning to direct serious attention to managerial manpower management? How much attention should be given to the academic community or specialists in planning techniques? Resolution of this audience problem has been to direct primary attention to organizations beginning their serious manpower management effort. However, it is felt that experienced manpower planners will find some of the ideas presented useful in their activities. In the academic community, those involved in the teaching of personnel management may be able to use material on labor productivity measurement and manpower forecasting in their classes. Resolving the audience problem in this manner will, it is hoped, result in more serious attention to manpower planning by the many organizations that should be concerned with the subject, and thus may mean some modest improvement in the utilization of our nation's manpower resources.

Initial data for the study were gathered from interviews with industrial manpower managers while the author was working on a doctoral dissertation at the University of Michigan. Subsequent research, consulting situations, and seminars provided additional facts. Varying amounts of information from over a hundred different companies have helped in the formulation of ideas. A debt of gratitude is acknowledged to the many unnamed individuals in industry who gave their time and aided the research effort.

Dr. George S. Odiorne, Director of the Bureau of Industrial Relations of the University of Michigan, has been a constant source of encouragement and ideas for the project. In addition, his Bureau helped to finance the initial research work. Several associates at Tulane University aided the author by commenting on individual chapters in the book; these include James T. Murphy, Clinton A. Phillips, Alfred Rappaport, and W. David Maxwell, now of Indiana University. In addition, Gerald Carvalho of the University of Michigan, Frank Tapparo of Tulane, and Ellis Wylie of the Michigan Bell Telephone Company offered many useful criticisms of the manuscript as a whole. These persons have helped to strengthen the material presented, but they cannot be responsible for any of its weaknesses or the failure of the author to use their criticisms as effectively as he should have.

The work of John Kendrick and Daniel Creamer for the National Industrial Conference Board in reporting upon the measurement of company productivity is acknowledged for its contribution to the discussion of that subject in Chapter 5. Their discussion of special problems in productivity measurement has been especially helpful in understanding the complexities of the task. No attempt has been made to duplicate their research efforts.

Appreciation is also due Mrs. Pamela Jendrek who typed many versions of the chapters and to Mrs. Ann Bernos and Mrs. Jeanette Warren, who also assisted in the typing. Graduate students Robert Davidson, Ronald Shrives, and Wayne Harper were helpful in assembling the bibliography.

Finally my wife, Ginny, deserves the special recognition due wives whose husbands engage in book writing — especially the writing of their first book. Her typing and editorial assistance has been very helpful. More significantly, she provided continued support and encouragement throughout the writing effort which appeared would never end. She also exhibited great patience when the book was sidetracked for other responsibilities.

CONTENTS

CHAPTER 1

THE NATURE OF MANAGERIAL MANPOWER PLANNING

There is nothing we can do about the performance of past management or the qualifications of today's management. But tomorrow's management can be as good as today's managers care to make it.
— RALPH BESSE

Early in the 1950's, Peter Drucker wrote about the importance of future manpower resources to a firm. He said, "The prosperity, if not the survival, of any business depends on the performance of its managers of tomorrow."[1]

The importance and implications of this statement are being increasingly recognized by responsible persons both in business and in other organizations who realize that the existence of an excellent management team does not happen by chance. Provision must be made for these managers long before they occupy their positions, for unless this is done, the organization may be left in the care of those not fully capable of managing it.

Although planning can be undertaken for all classes of employees, the focus in this book is on the managerial person. Our definition of a management person includes all those in the salaried-exempt wage classification. The concern is with the "high talent" manpower in the organization — the scientist, engineer, manager, and salesman — the group that makes most of the decisions and directs the welfare of the organization. It is this group for which planning is most important.[2]

The emphasis on "high talent" manpower in manpower planning activities does not mean that other employee groups are unimportant; all manpower in an organization requires attention and planning. With the high talent group, however,

[1] Peter F. Drucker, *The Practice of Management* (New York: Harper & Bros., 1954), p. 182.

[2] As Hill and Harbison have said, "Of all economic resources, high talent manpower takes the longest time to develop, and thus it demands the most careful consideration in planning for the future." Samuel E. Hill and Frederick Harbison, *Manpower and Innovation in America* (Princeton, New Jersey: Princeton University, 1959), p. 64.

the planning horizons tend to be longer because of the lead times required to effect changes in it. With hourly and clerical personnel, the planning horizon for a particular event is relatively short. If the company intends to go to two-shift production, for example, only two or three months of recruiting and selection work may be needed to build the necessary hourly workforce. If the company wishes to establish an overseas sales organization, however, it may need two or three years of lead time to obtain the desired quantity and quality of personnel.

Manpower is an asset which enables an enterprise to distinguish itself in performance from other enterprises. Manpower is more than a mere current resource used in the production process. It has a long economic life which deserves the same planning attention given to other assets with long lives. Actions taken today in the manpower area influence the quantity and quality of the company's future manpower.

Manpower planning, therefore, is concerned with the future, and involves establishing manpower objectives for the organization through an analysis of current and past events and by an attempt to forecast future events. Once established, action programs are designed to achieve these objectives.

With objectives determined and action programs designed, the organization is also better able to obtain internal consistency in decisions affecting the current manpower situation. Decisions in the college recruiting area, for example, can be better coordinated with decisions in the area of management development. In addition, because manpower planning activities are closely related to the overall profit objectives, their economic justification is seen more clearly.

WHAT IS MANPOWER PLANNING?

Manpower planning means different things to different organizations. To some companies, manpower planning means management development. It involves helping executives to make better decisions, communicate more effectively, and know more about the firm. The purpose is qualitative — to make men better managers. The emphasis is on having current managers (whatever their number) who are skilled in their functions and reasonably qualified for promotions. Too frequently the acquisition and development of the skills and knowledge needed for the future are lacking. The goal is often only to make the manager a better manager today.

The expenditure of large sums of money on management development in such cases does not insure a sound future manpower structure. Provision for the quantitative aspects of future management is not an essential part of such management development programs, yet without quantitative information on future manpower needs, the development programs cannot be geared to developing the numbers of managers who will be required in the future. Too, when management development programs are tied to short-range needs, they frequently fail to produce the qualitative product needed for the future.

In other firms, the approach to manpower planning is reversed. Here the problem is defined as estimating future manpower needs. The goal is to hire persons today to meet future requirements. The qualitative aspect of development is somehow to be met by a "natural" development process, even though future knowledge and skill requirements are ignored in the planning efforts. The guiding principle is to insure that enough "bodies" are available when needed. This quantitative-only approach is supported by a belief that the organization has never suffered because people were not capable — that manpower hardships can only result from a numerical manpower shortage.

Unfortunately, this type of thinking may exist because the organization does not evaluate the quality of its manpower carefully. A low managerial turnover rate may be considered to mean that managers are performing well. Another interpretation of the same statistic might be that these managers are not wanted by other firms and so are unable to relocate. The emphasis on numerical projections results in a lack of attention to necessary future managerial and professional qualities, to the level at which these qualities will be needed, or to the education and experience quotients that lead to the possession of these qualities. In addition, the lack of attention to qualitative problems may lead to the neglect of the career development of current managerial and professional personnel. Research in the aerospace industry, for example, indicates that many professional employees change jobs because of a neglect in manpower planning of these individual qualitative career factors.[3]

The problems posed by overemphasis on either quantitative or qualitative approaches are partially overcome by a third group of planners who define manpower planning as organization planning. Their approach is to code the current organization chart with color chips after each manager's name to indicate his current performance quality and his promotion potential. The planner then designs an "idealized" organization structure for some future time period. If a long-range organization plan (e.g., five years) is desired, the focus tends to be on higher management ranks because the planner lacks quantitative data on the probable structure and size of middle and lower management. If a detailed organization plan is desired, a short-run approach is adopted because of a lack of information on long-range needs.

Once the future organization is conceived, the planner allocates existing manpower to the future positions in view of their promotability, capability, and availability. This approach focuses attention on potential manpower problems due to the probable changes in the nature and structure of the organization. The planner tries to cope with external and internal forces at work on the organization which tend to make it behave in certain ways. Forces such as new markets, new production methods, and new competitive influences, for example, are considered.

Like the other two approaches to manpower planning, organization planning fails to provide the assurance that future manpower requirements are considered satisfactorily. The organization planner is restricted in his design work because of a lack of quantitative data, and because he does not have responsibility for programs that would develop managers to fill future organization positions.

Each of these approaches — management development, manpower forecasting, and organization planning — is inadequate by itself, yet each approach contains information needed for

---

[3] As yet unpublished results of interviews by the author with engineers and scientists at a large aerospace installation in 1966.

the other approaches. When combined with other aspects of manpower planning they become key links in an integrated manpower planning effort.

Our definition of manpower planning incorporates elements of all these approaches. It is defined as: *The process by which management determines how the organization should move from its current manpower position to its desired manpower position. Through planning, management strives to have the right number and the right kinds of people, at the right places, at the right time, doing things which result in both the organization and the individual receiving maximum long-run benefit.*

It is a four phased process. The first phase involves the gathering and analysis of data through *manpower inventories and forecasts*. The second phase consists of establishing *manpower objectives and policies* and gaining top management approval of these. The third phase involves designing and implementing *plans and action programs* in areas such as recruitment, training, and promotion to enable the organization to achieve its manpower objectives. The fourth phase is concerned with *control and evaluation* of manpower plans and programs to facilitate progress towards manpower objectives.

The emphasis in manpower planning is to benefit both the organization and the individual. The long-run view means that gains may be sacrificed in the short run for future benefits. The justification for the planning rests on economic grounds. The planning process enables the organization to identify what its manpower needs are and what potential manpower problems require current action. This leads to more effective and efficient performance.

Because of the economic rationale in manpower planning, the entire process should be carefully grounded in profit planning. Manpower planning is more than an interesting exercise in forecasting numbers, in managing the flow of managerial resources through the organization, or in introducing new personnel management methods. Manpower planning should result in benefits that justify its cost, or it should not be undertaken.

If manpower planning can yield a positive economic return, why isn't it more widely practiced? The answer probably rests in the amount of "felt pressure" for the activity in the past.

Although some firms have planned for manpower needs for many years, most companies have been able to achieve a reasonably satisfactory manpower structure without such planning. Increasingly, however, firms are feeling pressure on their ability to perform effectively. New strains are being placed on their manpower resources. The causes of this pressure? It is difficult to identify all of them. It appears, however, that perhaps the most fundamental reason is the current rate of increase in the production of knowledge — a rate that will increase in the future.

THE CURRENT NEED FOR MANPOWER PLANNING

Although many of the effects of new knowledge upon organizations are easily seen, the most important impact is the increased rate at which change takes place in the organization and its environment. Unless the firm is able to change successfully as its environment changes, it faces economic loss and possible extinction. In a competitive environment, economic strength is quickly lost by the company unable to keep pace with its rival. An ability to cope with changing conditions is usually a mark of the company which performs well economically. The awareness by higher management that economic success requires a workforce capable of adapting to new conditions leads to planning for that workforce.

The knowledge revolution is most clearly seen in the new products that result from advancing science and technology, but the effects are everywhere. They appear in the management area where decision-making models and advanced analytical approaches (e.g., simulation techniques) can result in a competitive advantage for their users. The insights gained by social scientists into the behavior of people and organizations under various conditions form another result of the knowledge revolution contributing to change in organizations. The quest for knowledge and some of the early findings are altering the attitudes of government bodies towards the social problems of communities, and are leading to legislation and government pressures on organizations to engage in a wide range of different practices. The business organization, too, must effectively adapt to these new pressures or suffer from its lack of flexibility.

The drive for new knowledge is spurred by researchers in industry, universities, and government. Each new finding opens avenues for further research and new applications. As this occurs, the business firm is forced to even more intense efforts in order to survive. Schumpeter's concept of "creative destruction"[4] serves as a driving force in research laboratories, offices, and computer centers across the nation. As competitors demonstrate ability to adapt to change and to initiate further change with new ideas, products, and methods, rivals face potential "destruction" unless they also develop new ways of creating demand, reducing costs, and serving society.

Today, changes to which much of the workforce has had little time to adapt are occurring. Compared with the past, competitive forces are now felt more keenly, economic opportunities appear more rapidly, and society is requiring better performance in economic and social areas. These pressures are causing managers to plan more carefully in the areas of finance, marketing, and production. The realization of the planning objectives in these areas is dependent upon the company's having the manpower resources that are implicit in the plans.

The pressures of change also result in a demand for new manpower skills and abilities. The utilization of new and different equipment to produce new products, and the need to operate in new markets, is shortening the life span of jobs. The change in demand for manpower skills is occurring more rapidly than many realize, and the prospect is for even greater changes in the future. As the authors of one study said, "It seems clear, however, that the American industrial system has not as yet experienced the full effect of automation since relatively little automation has occurred in the total American industrial scene. The full story of automation and job displacement has yet to unfold."[5]

The "Change Agents"

The knowledge revolution stimulates demand for the person

---

[4] Joseph A. Schumpeter, *Capitalism, Socialism and Democracy* (New York: Harper & Brothers, 1950), Chapter 7, "The Process of Creative Destruction."

[5] William Haber, Louis Ferman, and James R. Hudson, *The Impact of Technological Change* (Kalamazoo, Michigan: W. E. Upjohn Institute, 1963), p. 8.

who is capable of providing new knowledge and is able to convert knowledge into economic or social uses. This person can be considered the "agent of change" in the organization. He is found in the laboratory engaged in an analysis of chemical phenomena for new products, in the office studying the economic significance of the balance of payments on company investment decisions, and in the factory evaluating the feasibility of introducing new electronic control equipment. He is a "very high talent" person — whether scientist, engineer, or manager — who possesses specialized knowledge as well as the ability to utilize it within an organizational context.

A shortage of "very high talent" manpower cannot be met through intense company training because the knowledge required by these individuals is not quickly acquired. Offering premium salaries to attract them from other organizations may fail because they are relatively scarce and because money is only part of their personal complex motivation and reward system. In short, the organization must be increasingly concerned with insuring it has the necessary "very high talent" manpower it needs both to cope with change and to initiate change.

Professional Obsolescence

The formation rate of new knowledge has still another influence on manpower. The rapid advances in knowledge make it increasingly difficult for the professional man to maintain his proficiency. Returning experienced engineers and managers to the college classroom is the method by which some companies try to meet this problem. Other firms are doing nothing about it, sometimes because they are unaware of the growing obsolescence of their highly trained manpower. The unsolved problem of professional obsolescence posed by the production of knowledge is a threat to the growth potential of organizations and to the nation as a whole.

While the advance in knowledge generates forces that mean change in company manpower requirements, a sizable portion of the academic community lags behind in its teaching efforts. Educational institutions encourage the exploration of knowledge frontiers by the individual scholar and researcher, yet at the same time, many curricula are strongly tied to the past.

Most keenly felt at the secondary school level, this situation exists at all levels in our educational system. The problem arises in part from a lack of knowledge of how to communicate the "new knowledge" to students.

A more discouraging reason is the inability of many educators to recognize the need for curriculum change. Employers in all types of organizations should inform educators of their changing manpower needs; they should demand better prepared graduates — persons who are capable of coping with the future effectively. Manpower planning requires that the company look to the future to identify its future needs. Hopefully this looking will result in an improved exchange between the "real" world of work and the "academic" world of education with respect to the educational needs of society.[6]

THE STATISTICAL CASE FOR MANPOWER PLANNING

The pressure felt by all types of organizations to employ high talent manpower is also seen in a quantitative way. Historic trends show an increase in professional employment, and projections for the future show still greater increases. In addition, the next decade will be unusual because of the relative shortage of persons in the 35- to 44-year-old age group.

The Supply and Demand for Professional Manpower

Estimates of future national manpower needs point to the professional, technical, and kindred workers groups as the fastest growing occupational groups during the next ten years. Also projected is a large increase in managerial employees for the large and medium-size organization.[7] Table 1-1 shows the post-World War II growth in these two employment groups and estimates of future growth.

---

[6] An interesting and valuable source of information on this topic is in Fritz Machlup, *The Production and Distribution of Knowledge in the United States* (Princeton, New Jersey: Princeton University Press, 1962). See particularly Chapter 4, "Education," and Chapter 5, "Research and Development." See also, Gary S. Becker, *Human Capital*, National Bureau of Economic Research, General Series No. 80 (New York: Columbia University Press, 1964).

[7] Government statistics include proprietors of small business in the general classification of managerial employment. The number of proprietors is not expected to increase during the next decade. This means that the percentage growth of managers and officials of organizations will increase rather rapidly. See *Manpower Report of the President — 1965* (Washington, D.C.: Government Printing Office, 1965), p. 54.

TABLE 1-1

PROFESSIONAL AND MANAGERIAL EMPLOYMENT

(In Thousands)

	Professional, Kindred, and Technical Occupational Group		Managerial Occupational Group	
	Number Employed	Per Cent of Total Employment	Number Employed	Per Cent of Total Employment
1947	3,795	6.6	5,795	10.0
1950	4,490	7.5	6,429	10.8
1955	5,782	9.2	6,442	10.2
1960	7,475	11.2	7,067	10.6
1965	8,883	12.3	7,340	10.2
1970	11,000	13.5	8,400	10.3
1975	12,900	14.5	9,200	10.4

SOURCE: *Manpower Report of the President, 1967*, p. 211 and p. 274.

Statistics such as these, however, do not indicate what the relationship will be between the supply and demand for qualified persons. Making such estimates is admittedly difficult. Factors such as participation rates of older persons in the labor force, mobility into and out of occupational groups, the future role of the space program in our economy, use of women in managerial jobs, and utilization of those who enter the labor force without college degrees must be considered.

The 1965 *Manpower Report of the President* projected a probable balance of supply and demand for professional and related occupations through 1975. It added, however, that "In some fields, persistent personnel shortages are likely unless special efforts are made to increase the number of new entrants."[8] Science and engineering are given special attention in the yearly manpower reports because of possible shortages. In addition, any balance of supply and demand in professional occupations apparently will be achieved through the use of perhaps as many as 3,000,000 persons without college degrees.

During the early- and mid-1960's, the labor market for pro-

8 *Ibid.*, p. 114.

fessionals was greatly affected by the demands of the aerospace industry for highly trained manpower. For one large corporation, the competitive bidding for well-qualified persons pushed recruiting costs up to as high as $13,000 per engineering graduate hired. The rapid rise in starting salaries for engineers, scientists, and MBA's upset some salary administration systems. The differential between salaries paid new college hires and experienced manpower shrank because starting salaries rose faster than average salary increases for experienced personnel.

Government and Educational Demands for Manpower

Additional support for the statement of recent shortages of professional manpower is the large numbers of unfilled government positions for professional and managerial manpower. In New York City, for example, a study revealed that 20 per cent of the budgeted professional, managerial, and technical positions were unfilled and many others were filled by persons not fully qualified.[9]

Examination of available statistics indicates that under economic growth conditions, the future supply of those qualified for professional, technical, and managerial positions will, at best, barely satisfy the demand. Each new projection of employment in these occupational groups is usually greater than the previous projection.[10] Despite their own increased efforts and skill in college recruiting, business firms are finding government agencies and educational institutions more important as competitors in the labor market.

The demand by government agencies at all levels for planners, systems analysts, computer specialists, management scientists, health specialists, traffic engineers, social welfare experts, economists, and other professionals will grow rapidly in the next decade. The starting salaries for those positions, particularly those paid by federal agencies, are increasing; recruiting literature and techniques employed by many federal government groups now compare favorably with industry's efforts.

---

[9] *Ibid.*, p. 81.

[10] For example, the *Manpower Reports of the President* for 1964, 1965, and 1967, contained the following estimates of professional, technical, and kindred employment for 1975: 12,400,000; 12,750,000; and 13,000,000. In four years, therefore, the estimate for 1967 rose by 600,000 persons.

The impact of the government and universities on the supply of able manpower is summed up by the remarks of a personnel manager of a major chemical company which employs large numbers of scientists. He says:

> We're having a much more difficult time filling our requisitions for scientists. Not only have other firms stepped up their activity, but we find that the federal government is a much more effective bidder for talent than ever before. In addition, the top schools in the country are offering their Ph.D.'s a professorship combined with almost unlimited research money for projects of interest to Washington and financed by government money.

Another cause of this new labor market competition is disclosed by statistics. Institutions of higher education will need to replace about 320,000 professional staff members between 1965 and 1970. In addition, 250,000 more professionals will be needed for expansion purposes.[11] These requirements are currently acting as a stimulant to setting starting salaries to attract holders of advanced degrees to higher educational affiliations. A similar phenomenon is occurring with respect to the demand for elementary and secondary school teachers. It is estimated that 2,000,000 *new* teachers will be needed by these schools between 1965 and 1975.[12] Although the 1967 *Manpower Report of the President* indicates improvement in the supply of teachers, these demands will mean increased competition for the best talent available — especially as teaching wages improve.

Fewer Middle-aged Persons

The low birth rate during the 1930's means that the 35- to 44-year-old age group will be a relatively small one during the next ten years. In 1950, this group constituted over 14 per cent of the population; in 1970 it will represent 11 per cent; and by 1975 it will be less than 10 per cent. In actual numbers, it is estimated that there will be 800,000 fewer males in the workforce aged 35 to 44 in 1975 than there were in 1965. In addition, nearly two million fewer persons of both sexes in this age group will be in the population in 1975 than in 1965.[13]

What is the significance of this information to manpower planning? The 35- to 44-year-old age group is perhaps the

---

[11] *Manpower Report of the President — 1965, op. cit.,* p. 270.

[12] *Manpower Report of the President — 1967* (Washington, D.C.: Government Printing Office, 1967), p. 179.

[13] *Ibid.,* p. 268.

most important one in management staffing. Men in this group have ten to 20 years of experience in specialized and varied assignments, which result in abilities that cannot be learned in the classroom: a sharpening of decision-making skills, an ability to live with mistakes, and a growth in self-confidence as a result of past successes. This kind of management talent, which is especially important to an organization as it tries to cope successfully with the demands of change, is also the kind of experience that must be gained by men selected for top management. And it is from the 35- to 44-year-old age group that most of the new top managers appointed in the 1970's will be selected.

Some organizations have discovered that this age distribution factor already poses a problem. During the depression years of the 1930's, these firms were trying to protect current managers' jobs and did little, if any, hiring. Manpower shortages in World War II meant another five years of reduced hiring of young management talent. These factors have combined with a short supply of middle-aged men to create staffing problems. As retirements in the late 1960's and early 1970's drain off personnel hired during the 1920's, these firms will lack men with adequate experience to move into higher level vacancies.

Because many organizations are short of experienced manpower, it is increasingly difficult to recruit capable men in this age group. Their short supply inside an organization increases their opportunities for promotion there and lowers their desire to relocate. At the same time, the organization that does not utilize men in this age group intelligently may find them leaving because of opportunities elsewhere.

INVESTMENT IN HUMAN RESOURCES

Another, and very compelling, reason for manpower planning is the investment an organization makes in its manpower resources. Unlike most other assets of the company, manpower can increase in value through utilization. In fact, the more intensively it is utilized with respect to its capability and capacities, the more valuable it tends to become. A manager who is forced to use his abilities to the fullest develops into an even better manager. The manager operating below his capacity in a non-challenging assignment, however, may depreciate in value through a lack of use.

This fact that manpower is an asset that can appreciate through careful utilization is another argument for manpower planning. A manpower plan that increases the value of manpower has demonstrable economic returns. Such a plan might involve planned job assignments of those managers with promotion potential. Placing men in positions to provide necessary experience for future positions is an investment in them, even though it may entail reduced short-run efficiency. But highly qualified and experienced top executives are needed to make future major resource and policy decisions.

Because an organization makes investments in its personnel either through direct training or job assignments, it is important that employees are utilized effectively throughout their careers. Computer information retrieval systems may effectively identify manpower with the proper qualifications for particular assignments. This facilitates their placement on the basis of skill and ability — something which is often not possible when the organization is ineffective in screening its personnel records manually.

Decisions on the assignment of manpower can be regarded from an opportunity-cost point of view. By placing a manager in a particular job the planner sacrifices the opportunity of that manager's being in another position where he might perform better or where he might better learn and develop for future utilization. In the same vein, the planner sacrifices the opportunity of having another person in the position in order to realize the learning and development opportunities that exist in the position.

The dollar value of a trained, flexible, motivated, and productive workforce is difficult to determine. The quality of the workforce, however, can be responsible for significant differences in the short- and long-run performances among firms. Money may enable a company to duplicate a competitor's physical facilities, but money cannot enable a company to duplicate the quality of a competitor's manpower. Needed for that, in addition to money, is a management that recognizes the asset role of manpower and is willing to make provision for future manpower.[14]

CONCLUSION

As Ralph Besse of the Cleveland Electric Illuminating Company once said, "There is nothing we can do about the performance of past management or the qualifications of today's management. But tomorrow's management can be as good as today's managers care to make it."[15] This helps to sum up the need for manpower planning.

A final benefit results from the activity. In providing good management for the future, the organization also better services society. Its improved overall economic performance and its better utilization of scarce manpower resources are direct results. Its development of information of value to educators developing entrants to the labor force is another result. As important a benefit as any is the increased opportunity for individuals to utilize their special talents and to find self-expression in their work.

A great deal of manpower planning attention is directed toward individual managers. Enriching the opportunities for individual growth and development is a major objective of manpower planning. To have managers correctly placed in the organization on the basis of both present and future organizational considerations, careful attention must be given to the individual and his needs. In this area of manpower planning, the behavioral scientist contributes significantly. His understanding of motivation, personality, attitudes, and organization behavior is helpful in successfully integrating the needs of the individual with the needs of the organization.

Success in manpower planning is not seen in the accuracy

---

[14] The idea of investment in human resources was given impetus by Theodore W. Schultz of the University of Chicago. Dr. Schultz' interest has been in the investment the nation as a whole makes in its manpower resources through education and other programs including company-sponsored or supported training and education. See, T. W. Schultz, "Capital Formation by Education," *Journal of Political Economy* (December, 1960), 571-583; and "Investment in Human Capital," *American Economic Review* (March, 1961), 1-17. Rensis Likert develops the asset role of manpower in small organization units in his *New Patterns of Management* (New York: McGraw-Hill Book Company, 1961).

[15] Ralph M. Besse, "Tomorrow's Managers." Address before the Edison Electric Institute, New York, June 7, 1961.

of a manpower forecast or in the uniqueness of an action program. The use of forecasts, objectives, and programs helps in the identification and avoidance of serious manpower problems. Success, instead, is measured by whether the organization has the management personnel it requires when needed. This is both a quantitative consideration and a qualitative one.

CHAPTER 2

THE MANPOWER PLANNING PROCESS

Reliance on random development...is a do-nothing policy which involves the misconception that in the ordinary course of enterprise activity, candidates who possess management potential will "obviously" emerge from the ranks in sufficient numbers at the right time.
— HAROLD KOONTZ and CYRIL O'DONNELL

Like other planning activities, manpower planning is based on the formulation of objectives to provide guidance and direction for the programs. They are related to the planner's understanding of future economic demands on the organization and to the implications of these demands on the manpower structure.

The quality of the objectives tends to improve as knowledge of the future improves. In the manpower area this knowledge is gained in part through a forecast of future manpower requirements. To make successful forecasts is not easy because the further ahead forecasts are attempted, the more difficult the task becomes.

To improve the quality of the manpower forecast the planner must try to understand both the factors that have influenced the past as well as the current manpower structure. He must examine historical manpower statistics and consult with managers throughout the organization.

Such factors help to govern the preliminary planning process. The ability to cope with them and to integrate them into the planning process will vary with the nature and needs of each organization and with its acceptance of a manpower planning philosophy.

In one sense the procedure for manpower planning outlined below is a plan to guide the manpower planning effort. It is presented to focus attention upon important key steps in manpower planning. Although this planning process may not fit the needs of any one organization, awareness of the need for a systematic approach to planning is important. The ideas in the chapter may prove useful to the person responsible for planning, for it cannot be too strongly emphasized that the manpower planner should use a planning system in his work.

AN OVERVIEW OF THE PROCESS

Long-range manpower planning activities can be classified into four phases: the first involves data collection and analytical work which lead to a manpower inventory and a manpower forecast; the second involves the identification of manpower problems and the determination of long-range manpower policies and objectives; the third consists of designing and implementing manpower plans and programs to secure long-range objectives; and the fourth is program control and evaluation of the performance of the plans and programs in relation to their objectives.

The basic economic, sales, and growth objectives of the firm are essential data inputs to the process. These estimates help define the path of activities that the organization should undertake in the future. The manpower planner accepts the objectives set by top management in these areas. Because he uses them, however, he should know how they are developed, the assumptions they rest upon, their probable accuracy, and reasons for possible departure from them.

Figure 2-1 shows the manpower planning process. The overall corporate objectives, policies, and plans influence the entire process. These corporate considerations, however, are in turn influenced by information gathered in Phase I. The manpower inventory tells the organization its current manpower capability and this influences what the organization is capable of achieving. The manpower forecast may reveal factors that influence the desirability of certain corporate goals and the probability of achieving these goals.

With a manpower inventory and forecast, and an understanding of corporate objectives, policies, and plans, the planner is able to set manpower objectives and policies. These

FIGURE 2-1

THE MANPOWER PLANNING PROCESS

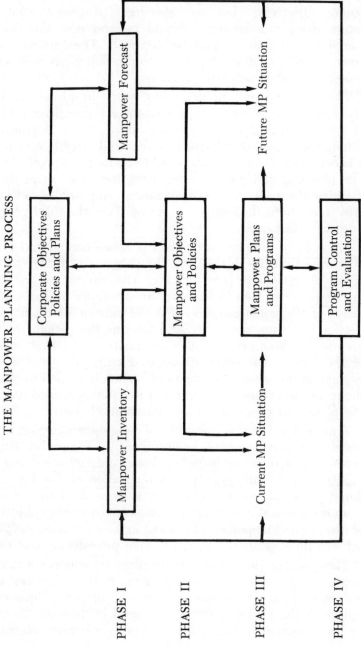

objectives and policies may create a need to re-examine corporate objectives. They will also help to govern what the
future manpower situation should be and how the current
manpower situation should be managed. Their primary use,
however, is to enable the planner to develop plans and action
programs in the manpower area.

The planning and programming work in Phase III may
also cause a retracing of steps and suggest a need for revision
of the overall manpower objectives and policies. Whenever a
situation is probed deeply and new data and insights are gained,
it is necessary to examine the need to revise previous decisions.
The planning and programming work has as its main thrust,
however, the movement of organization manpower from its current status to its desired future status. Thus the third phase is
primarily time oriented.

Phase IV of the process involves program control and evaluation to inform the planner on the progress and effectiveness
of his planning and programming. The information gathered
in this phase is used to maintain an inventory on the current
status of the organization so that the current situation is understood as time passes. It also informs the planner on the
accuracy of his forecast and his estimate of the likely nature
of the future manpower situation. Finally, the control and
evaluation phase tells the planner if action is needed to change
the manpower plans or programs or if action is needed to cause
the plans and programs to become more effective.

A more developed relationship of manpower planning to the
general economic goals of the firm is seen in Figure 2-2. Higher
ordered objectives are linked to lower ordered ones, and the
higher ones are attained from a realization of the lower ordered ones. Manpower planning is several steps removed
from the survival, return on investment, and growth objectives
of the firm. Manpower planning, in other words, helps to
achieve these goals but does not take precedence over them.

This point of view in manpower planning is important. Adequate manpower is an enabling factor in the achievement of
economic goals — it is not a primary objective. Success or
failure of the planning is not measured by forecast accuracy
or by program sophistication. When economic objectives

FIGURE 2-2

THE RELATIONSHIP OF MANPOWER PLANNING
TO ECONOMIC OBJECTIVES

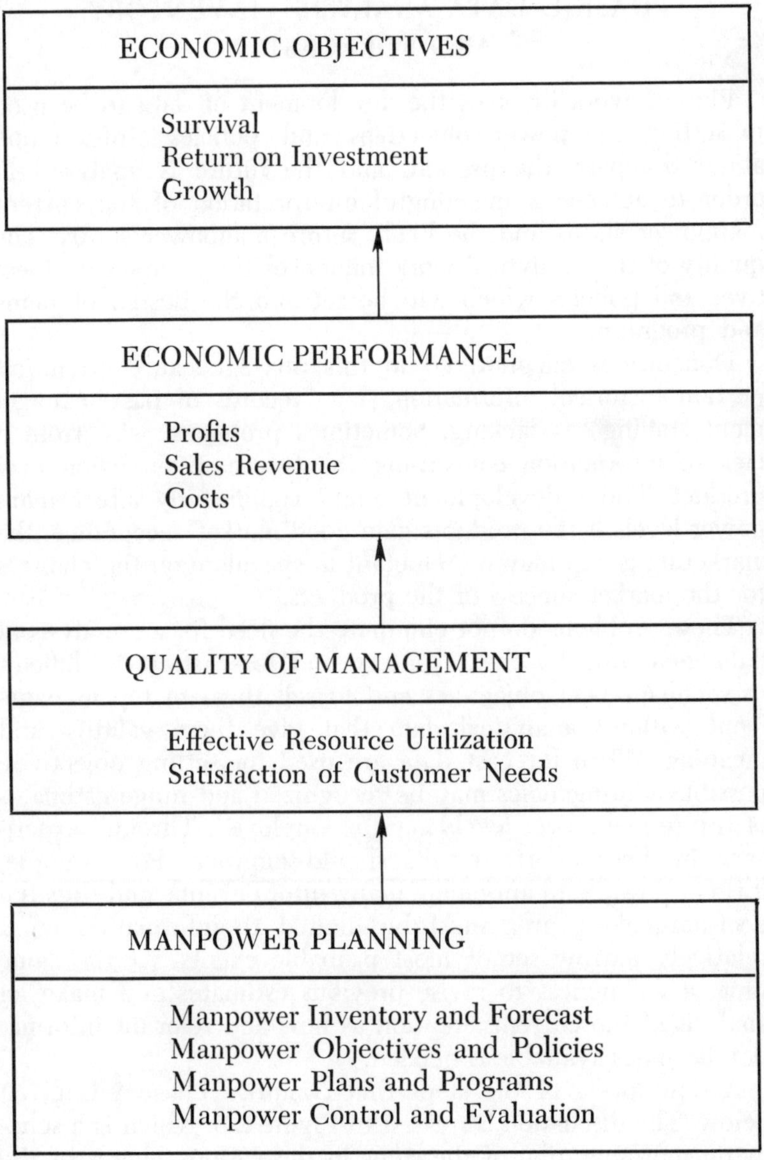

ECONOMIC OBJECTIVES

Survival
Return on Investment
Growth

ECONOMIC PERFORMANCE

Profits
Sales Revenue
Costs

QUALITY OF MANAGEMENT

Effective Resource Utilization
Satisfaction of Customer Needs

MANPOWER PLANNING

Manpower Inventory and Forecast
Manpower Objectives and Policies
Manpower Plans and Programs
Manpower Control and Evaluation

change, manpower requirements may change. For this reason, the accuracy of the manpower forecast is significant only as it assists in the acquistion and effective utilization of manpower.

PHASE I: DATA ANALYSIS – INVENTORY AND FORECAST

Phase I work involves the development of data to be used in setting manpower objectives and policies. Information about the past, the present, and the future is analyzed in order to achieve a meaningful interpretation of the current manpower status and the likely future manpower status. The quality of this analytical work influences the manpower objectives and policies which will be set and the design of plans and programs.

Difficulty is encountered in this phase because often important historical information (e.g., records of past management staffing) is lacking. Sometimes problems arise from a lack of information concerning the future. Even when new products under development might significantly affect manpower levels if the products gain good market acceptance, the marketing group may be reluctant to speculate on the chances for the market success of the products.

These problems do not eliminate the need for an analysis of data generated by the inventory and forecast. It is difficult to set manpower objectives and to sell them to top management without analytical data that give them validity and meaning. When forecast data are used for setting objectives, possible contingencies may be recognized and range estimates of future manpower levels may be employed. Through experience in these efforts, results should improve. For example, it is not possible to anticipate many future events, and thus the decision-making area must be limited to information on a relatively narrow set of most probable events. At the same time, a willingness to revise previous estimates and make an analysis of the current situation as new and relevant information becomes available is needed.

A description of the steps that comprise Phase I is given below. The discussion is related to Figure 2-3, which is a schematic representation of the steps in the various phases of the manpower planning process. Paragraph numbers in the text relate to the activities shown on the diagram.

Step 1: Analysis of the Manpower Situation

An analysis of several current and historical variables related to the organization's manpower situation is the first step in the planning process. Four key areas require attention.

a) An inventory of the current management manpower of the organization is undertaken to determine the capability of the current management team. Information on the age, experience, skills, performance quality, and promotion potential of managers is assembled and analyzed. The data help provide an initial statement of the ability of the organization to meet current and future responsibilities and are examined with respect to future management manpower needs in Step 5.[1]

b) An analysis of past occupational employment trends is made to assist in estimating the probable future composition of the workforce. This study involves an analysis of employment by basic wage groups (e.g., hourly, salaried-exempt, and salaried non-exempt personnel), and by occupational groups (e.g., scientific, engineering, managerial, sales, etc.). In some organizations, an analysis of employment trends by sex may be important because of the number of females employed.

c) An analysis of past labor productivity is made to determine the increase in labor efficiency over time. Although the emphasis is on labor productivity, examination of fixed capital utilization aids in understanding the factors leading to increased labor efficiency and provides a basis for projecting future labor productivity which is a key element in manpower forecasting.

d) The future organizational structure influences total manpower requirements. The design will influence manpower allocation and the general composition of the management team. The manpower planner needs more than information on past organization changes and forseeable future changes. He needs

---

[1] The undertaking of this analysis is especially important as an initial step when manpower planning efforts are first undertaken. Once manpower planning has become an ongoing activity in the organization, this analysis may be made a part of Step 5. In this book, facets of the analysis are discussed in Chapter 3 and in Chapter 4 where several manpower inventory and forecast data are integrated through the use of tables.

FIGURE 2-3
A PROCEDURE FOR MANPOWER PLANNING

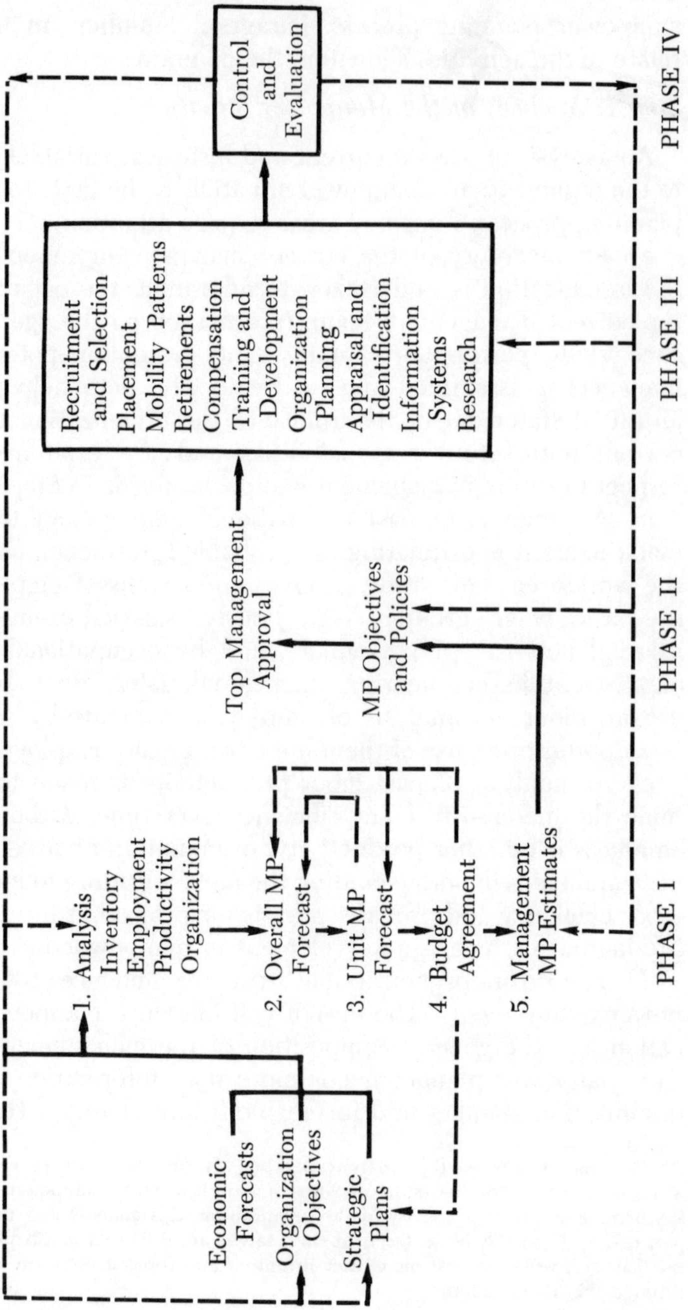

an estimate of the probable relative size of the top, middle, and lower management levels, as well as information on activities that are expected to experience major growth or contraction.

Step 2: Forecast of Total Manpower Needs

The data collected in the analysis steps are integrated with the general economic forecasts to make an overall manpower forecast for the organization. Projected labor productivity is related to the forecast of total output in order to estimate total manpower, which is then broken down into wage and occupational groups.

Step 3: Unit Manpower Forecasts

Estimates of unit manpower needs are based on information from the organization study and information furnished by the units. Since the unit estimates when summed may not equal the estimate of total manpower made from the productivity data, reconcilation of the two sub-totals is necessary before further planning work can be undertaken. The total manpower forecast may also need revision because of the information received from the units (shown as a broken line from Step 3 to Step 2 in Figure 2-3), or the unit estimates may need revision in view of the overall forecast.

Step 4: Budget Reconcilation

A critical step in the planning process is comparison of the manpower estimates with the firm's future financial plans, for it it essential that the manpower forecast be expressed in terms of dollars compatible with the company's profit objectives. When projected labor expenses are compared with projected budgeted expenses, revisions in the manpower estimates may be needed to fit budget limitations. Equally significant may be the fact that the financial estimates are unrealistic in light of manpower considerations. The broken line in Figure 2-3 leading from the budget agreement step to stragetic plans shows that revisions may be required in the profit plans. The budget agreement thus provides added realism to both the manpower and the financial projections.

Step 5: Management Manpower Estimates

A detailed examination of the management manpower requirements is then undertaken. Inventory information gathered in Step 1-A is combined with manpower forecast data to identify problems in the college recruiting, management development, promotion and transfer, and general areas of manpower utilization. The manpower planner makes this analysis for the management group as a whole. In addition, analyses by organizational units of their own "high talent" situations and future requirements are desired to further the units' understanding of their individual planning responsibilities.

PHASE II: SETTING OBJECTIVES AND POLICIES

Objectives and policies for the manpower planning period can now be established; they provide operational meaning to the analytical work. One such objective might be to have 150 qualified middle managers properly placed in five years, even though only 100 persons at present appear to be available for such duties. Another objective might be to prevent total manpower costs from rising by more than ten per cent annually, including provision for additional staffing. A third objective might involve reducing the turnover rate of new college hires in their first five years of service from 50 per cent to 30 per cent in order to lower costs and meet future manpower needs.

Consideration needs to be given to the impact of the objectives on other activities of the enterprise. The relationship of these long-range objectives to short-run management problems and situations should be considered to help the planner to set realistic short-run goals and to design and administer plans and programs.

It is also necessary to examine the basic policies that govern the manpower effort in the organization. Policies are broad guidelines which are related to objectives and which set the outer boundaries of decision-making freedom. They affect all aspects of the manpower effort and although they frequently may seem to lack operational meaning they do provide structure to the environment. An example of a policy that may need attention is that of rigid promotion from within that supports the managerial motivation system. Analysis of inventory and forecast data may suggest manpower objectives that indicate such a promotion policy requires revision. Other policies requiring attention might concern mandatory or optional retirement age for managers, or whether to treat all new hires from college campuses in an identical manner or whether to impose differential treatment based on apparent potential and demonstrated past performance in college. Thus, the examination and definition of policies is important to the success of manpower plans and programs.

Before engaging in the specifics of designing plans and programs, top management should approve the manpower objectives and policies that will guide the plans and programs. Top management should also approve the assumptions that support the manpower forecast and the objectives. The briefing for top management should rest on a sound analysis of the current manpower situation and defensible assumptions regarding the future. Without top management approval of the planning effort, the ability of the planner to take action to solve problems and meet future requirements is severely restricted. The planner should not expect, however, that because higher management approves a general set of objectives and the overall direction of the planning effort, that he has been given *carte blanche* authority to implement his plans. Higher management is more likely to approve moving ahead with the overall effort within the confines of the existing authority and influence structure of the organization.

PHASE III: ACTION PROGRAMMING

That planning objectives and manpower forecast data guide in designing plans and action programs in a wide variety of areas is also indicated in Figure 2-3. Specialists familiar with the activities of the organization in these areas will be utilized to modify existing programs or to design new programs to meet manpower goals.

Manpower planning can result in three major improvements in the normal programming work. First, the establishment of a planning period with end-of-period objectives and goals results in an overall, or umbrella, time horizon for the design of action programs. This means that the coordination of activities is improved and the programs are less likely to conflict with one another, as can occur, for example, when the salary administration program is not clearly related to the development and performance evaluation programs of management.

The second major improvement is the pressure manpower planning generates for action in areas that might otherwise be neglected. Attempts can be made to reach a target management staffing level through recruiting and by reducing attrition. The recognition of control over the attrition rate as a key factor in reaching staffing goals may require compilation of information on manager attitudes — especially the attitudes of recent hires because of a high early attrition rate.

A third planning benefit is the greater incentive it generates to develop and design individualized programs, to rely less on the adoption of programs developed by other persons or, for example, upon the philosophy and objectives of a successful performance evaluation program developed in some other company. The planner must conceive and design a program which serves his company's own planning objectives. The appraisal program must yield more than mere evaluation information. It must provide the management development expert with information on what he should be doing. It should also provide information for the college recruiters on the type of manpower they need to recruit, and should assist the salary administrator in designing salary maturity curves and establishing salary classifications. The fact that manpower objectives affect more than one action program area means that borrowed concepts and programs are less likely to be successful if introduced from another organization.

Examples of action planning programs are given in the next chapter. The experience of these firms is not that of unqualified successes in their ventures but an awareness of objectives in the design of the programs, and a long-range attitude towards manpower problems characterizes their efforts.

PHASE IV: PROGRAM CONTROL AND EVALUATION

Success in manpower planning is dependent upon the control system used to monitor performance. To increase the quality of performance, the planner needs to review his work regularly and to identify causes of positive and negative deviations from his plans.

In manpower planning an end-of-year review is important. Prior to the analysis and decision-making that leads to the setting of new manpower objectives, a critical evaluation of past performance is helpful. This evaluation can result in the identification of information to improve manpower forecasting techniques and can reveal defects in the hypotheses and logic in the design of action programs. In general, such a review improves the overall capability of the planner for his work.

In addition to year-end sessions, control procedures help pilot the plan through time. The tracking of actual manpower levels against target levels reveals deviations as they occur. Either corrective action is required to achieve the target levels or revisions must be made in the targets.

The controls established will vary in formality and complexity. Staffing level programs are easier to evaluate than those related to management development because of problems in obtaining objective information on the success of training. A written progress report by the college recruiter might be an adequate control device for that activity. In salary administration, however, statistical evaluation of the distribution of wages by salary grade, departments, and job classifications may be desired.

Related to control is evaluation. To understand the implications of the data for decision-making, information generated by the control monitoring system must be understood. The development of an "evaluative mentality" is necessary. This mentality refuses to be satisfied with the status quo; it seeks improvement and looks for defects in existing systems. It results in new ideas and fresh thinking. It operates at all times — not only during year-end reviews. (Additional discussion of this phase is given in Chapter 8.)

ORGANIZATIONAL UNIT MANPOWER PLANNING RESPONSIBILITIES

The manpower planning program benefits greatly when operating units are actively involved in the entire project. Manpower forecasts are improved when information that otherwise might not be available is obtained from the units. The objectives set are more realistic when there is first-hand knowledge of individual unit needs. Furthermore, action programs may contain fewer mistakes when unit personnel have had a hand in their design. Control procedures also work better when those affected by them have had an opportunity to examine them before they are placed into operation. Participation, in general, raises the acceptance level of the manpower planning task by the entire organization.

One of the major potential benefits of any planning exercise thus is the understanding that it generates throughout the organization. The identification of problems and the setting of objectives help to draw personnel together in terms of the common challenges they face. In the process of reaching agreement upon goals and objectives, potential organizational conflicts tend to come to the surface. Joint efforts in designing action programs reveal the interdependency of organization elements and thus lead to greater awareness of the overall systems and of the nature of the organization.

The challenge facing the manpower planner is how to succeed in involving units in the planning effort. Premature involvement may lead to discouragement and a loss of respectability of the program. Failure to involve a unit means a loss of an opportunity to generate understanding of the manpower problems in the firm and to possible resentment over not having been consulted.

Utilization of a manpower coordinator in each significant organizational unit is a workable means of gaining department involvement. The coordinator serves his unit as a manpower expert and troubleshooter. He furnishes data on past and future staffing needs and problems. In addition to helping implement action programs in his unit, he works with other department coordinators on a manpower planning committee that meets to generate overall plans and programs for the organization.

The role of these unit coordinators in the manpower forecast is enhanced when they are given guidance on how to perform their work. They need guidance on the general methodology used to forecast manpower, and briefing on company economic and sales goals, budget considerations, future production activities, wage trend information, and a general overview of corporate strategy. The forecasts of the individual coordinators are used to finalize the overall manpower forecast for the company. These individual forecasts should include an explanation and defense of the hypotheses made by the coordinators in their forecasts. This information is needed by the company's major manpower planner to interpret the data he receives intelligently and to evaluate the understanding and acceptance by the organization of the manpower planning program.

When a manpower planning program is introduced, there may not be persons in the departments who are qualified to serve as the unit coordinator. This will mean that the initial unit involvement may be less than it becomes at later stages. In the initial situation, the overall manpower planner may make many forecasts and plans with little involvement of the units. He gains experience on availability of data, forecasting problems, and organizational acceptance of the program to guide his future use of unit coordinators. Such an initial debugging period in manpower planning may increase the later acceptance of the program.

Thus, despite the desirability of full unit involvement in manpower planning, the lack of a capability of the units to furnish data and to discharge program responsibilities may dictate a modified approach during the early program stages. Because manpower planning effectiveness is dependent upon the cooperation and support of managers throughout the organization, its introduction obviously requires careful thought. The involvement of units should be related to their ability to respond adequately to their information and coordination role in manpower planning.

DETERMINING THE PLANNING PERIOD

Another important consideration in manpower planning is the length of the time period to plan against. Determination of the planning period involves two major considerations. The most basic criterion is that the period will provide the organization with adequate time to make necessary adjustments to potential problems and needs as revealed by the forecast. With managerial manpower this usually means a five-year planning period. For most companies, five years provides sufficient lead time for recruitment, development, and organizational planning; permits gradual adjustments to future conditions; and does not require a forecast too far into the future.

The second major criterion in establishing the planning period is that it relate effectively to the other major activities of the firm. Coordination and integration of data and programs of various plans are needed to increase planning effectiveness. It is difficult to evaluate the impact of the manpower plan on profits unless both plans are for the same time period. Further, manpower forecasts require the use of forecast data on output. Since these data are usually furnished by other planners, their availability is related to the time period used by those planners.

An exception to the second criterion is made when factors relating to the first criteria dominate. This occurs when a manpower problem requires a longer lead time for solution than is allowed by the normal planning period, when for example, unusually large numbers of middle and top managers are scheduled to retire after the normal planning period. Replacing the retirees may require more time than the planning period had allowed. When this happens, a separate manpower forecast and plan must be made to help meet the situation, in addition to the manpower plan relating to the overall company plans. A retirement problem is the reason some companies have made forecasts and plans for management needs as far as fifteen years ahead.

The long-run planning period provides the common time coverage for manpower activities. It has been seen how this assists in the action programming phase of manpower planning. It is also important to recognize that these action programs will also involve shorter planning periods. The short-run period, however, frequently involves activities that should be geared to longer-run considerations. College recruiting, for example, may involve a one-year planning period in terms of campus visitations, but the number of men recruited from the campuses in any year should be related to the intake needs of a longer period. Similarly, management development activities may be recycled every two years, although their ultimate payoff is in the more distant future.

A variety of planning periods will therefore exist in man-power planning. The long-term period provides the needed common time horizon for the setting of objectives and general planning. Within this period, shorter periods (e.g., one year) are utilized to realize immediate, short-term objectives and to guide the action programs. The shorter-run objectives also serve as milestones for evaluation of current performance against the long-run plan.[2]

The general planning activities, however, are updated annual-ly, or more frequently if the corporate objectives and environ-ment change sufficiently to affect manpower needs significantly. In the annual updating another year is added to the forecast. This permits modification of manpower plans to accommodate new demands on the organization. It also permits a long-term approach to be made to manpower problems.

THE NECESSARY INFORMATION SYSTEM

In developing a manpower planning program, attention should be given to the information system that will be needed to service the program. The planner needs to determine what information will be required, what information is currently available, and how he can best collect new data. In this analy-sis, he attempts to eliminate collection and reporting of man-power data that are no longer useful. New reports should re-place or consolidate existing reports whenever possible.

The quality of the initial Phase I analytical work may be below desired levels because of the lack of historical informa-tion, but as the information system matures this problem is gradually overcome. One of the concerns in designing the in-formation system is identification of information which the planner might wish to analyze at some future date. If he collects current data in gross terms (i.e., without much discrimination in the composition of the data) he may discover later that his analytical work is hampered. An example might be the reasons engineers give for voluntary separations from the company. If discrimination between controllable and uncontrollable factors

---

[2] For an interesting discussion of long-range planning see: George A. Steiner (ed.), *Managerial Long-Range Planning* (New York: McGraw-Hill Book Com-pany, 1963). Also see Peter F. Drucker, "Long Range Planning — Challenge to Management Science," *Management Science* (April 1959), 238-249.

is impossible because of a lack of categories for termination reasons, later analyses will be adversely affected.

Another consideration in the design of the information system is the burden it places on the organization. If operating units are solicited for excessive amounts of data, they may reduce their cooperation and become unresponsive to the requests. The information gathering system, therefore, should be carefully constructed to stimulate a responsive and smooth flow of data.

The manpower planner should constantly evaluate the information system. He may be able to computerize much of the data and relieve departments of many reporting duties, or to simplify the report forms or design them to provide information useful to the reporting unit as well as to the manpower planning group. Finally, he should evaluate the data received regularly to determine their accuracy and validity as bases for decision-making.

CONCLUSION

A well-conceived manpower planning procedure will not guarantee success in the activity. The procedure does not, by itself, guarantee good analytical work or the acceptance of the manpower planning approach to problems. A sound system will, however, enable the planner to avoid omitting some important steps in his work and it will provide structure and guidance to his efforts. To know what should be accomplished and why it should be accomplished, the manpower planner must develop his planning procedure before he begins his actual planning work.

THE MANPOWER PLANNING PROCEDURE OF AN AEROSPACE FIRM

The manpower planning procedure discussed in this chapter is similar in several respects to one used by a division of a large aerospace firm. The procedure used in this firm is outlined below to indicate the scope of the task one organization has established for itself.[1]

Because of the unstable nature of the government work done in this firm, forecasts are made for two types of business activity. The first is a long-range forecast based on known or highly probable business (Type I Business). The second forecast is based on business which is as yet unknown or quite uncertain at the time of the forecast (Type II Business).

Step I in the procedure (Figure 2-4) is for the planning staff to make a five-year business program summary. This is transmitted with forms and procedures furnished by the manpower planning group (MPG), to functional and operational units, which then forecast direct manpower requirements against Type I Business (Step 2). This information is sent to the MPG which prepares total manpower forecasts for direct labor requirements (Step 3). The planning group consults with the finance department before final estimates are made by the MPG (Step 4).

Responsibility now shifts to the finance department for preparation of indirect manpower requirements of the Type I Business. Functional and operational units prepare indirect manpower forecasts using the five-year business summary and the approved direct manpower requirements as their guides (Step 5). The finance department approves these forecasts after consultation with the MPG (Step 6), which assembles the

---

[1] To facilitate exposition the description of this planning procedure is a slight modification of the actual procedure used.

FIGURE 2-4

PROCEDURE OF MANPOWER FORECASTING
AN AEROSPACE FIRM – TYPE I BUSINESS

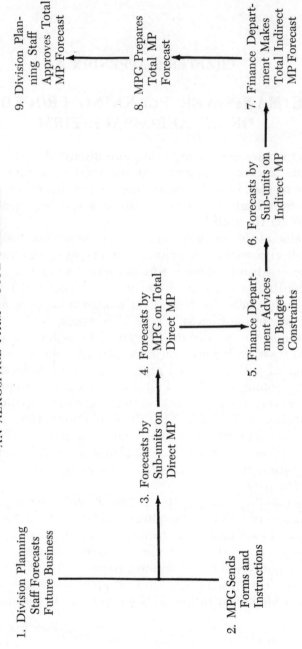

Diagram of the information flow and procedural relations used in manpower forecasting for Type I (known) business of an aerospace firm.

total forecast (Step 7) and sends it to the planning staff for approval (Step 8).

Once the Type I Business manpower estimates are made, work begins on the Type II Business manpower forecast. The planning staff and the MPG prepare this forecast with the assistance of the functional departments. Final estimates are reviewed for internal consistency and approval is gained from the managers involved. The planning staff approves the final plan, as is shown in Figure 2-5.

Under this procedure, the MPG and the finance department provide advice, assistance, and coordination to the other departments in the organization. Disagreement over manpower estimates are settled before the forecasts are sent to the planning staff. The MPG is responsible for forms, instructions, and completion dates of the forecasts. A five-year time schedule is prepared to insure that reports are submitted when required. The forecasts are complex and detailed. Some of the information furnished in the reports is listed below:

1. Estimates are made for both certain and unknown business.

2. Manpower estimates are made for both direct and indirect personnel.

3. Estimates are made for approximately ten major product groups, a research program, and for miscellaneous activities.

4. Manpower is estimated on a monthly basis for the first year of the program and on a quarterly basis for the remaining four years.

5. New four-quarter estimates are required each quarter and new five-year estimates are made each year.

6. Manpower is forecast for departments, organizations within departments, and for more than 20 geographical locations.

7. Seventeen professional and scientific skill groups, two non-exempt salaried classes, a special payroll, and an hourly payroll are included in the forecast.

8. Past actual and forecast totals are charted and explanations furnished on deviations of the actual from the forecast totals.

The data developed in this system are used in recruiting,

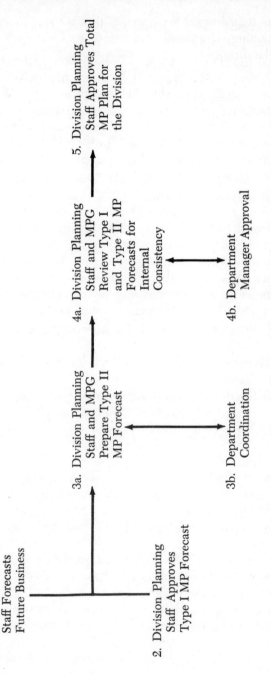

FIGURE 2-5

PROCEDURE OF MANPOWER FORECASTING
AN AEROSPACE FIRM – TYPE II BUSINESS

1. Division Planning Staff Forecasts Future Business

2. Division Planning Staff Approves Type I MP Forecast

3a. Division Planning Staff and MPG Prepare Type II MP Forecast

3b. Department Coordination

4a. Division Planning Staff and MPG Review Type I and Type II MP Forecasts for Internal Consistency

4b. Department Manager Approval

5. Division Planning Staff Approves Total MP Plan for the Division

Diagram of the information flow and procedural relations used in manpower forecasting for Type II (unknown) business of an aerospace firm.

equipment ordering, floor space allocation, manpower allocation, training, overhead budgeting, and future business program planning.

A MANPOWER PLANNING CHECKLIST

To evaluate the current status of the manpower management programs in an organization, the following checklist may prove useful. The list does not cover all aspects of manpower management; it does serve as a departure point for the development of an evaluation system related to the needs of a particular organization. The objective of the procedure is to help identify areas where manpower management is weak and where planning is required. Rate each statement through the use of the rating scale below.

1. — Our effort needs a great deal of improvement.
2. — Our effort has room for a good deal of improvement.
3. — Our effort is generally adequate (except in a few spots).
4. — Our effort is good — no real weaknesses.
5. — Our effort is outstanding — we stay on top of it.

—— Maintaining an adequate information system on management manpower.
—— Anticipating future managerial manpower requirements.
—— Recruiting the desired number of well-qualified young men from college.
—— Effectively placing newly hired young managers to make them productive.
—— Adequately evaluating the current performance of managers.
—— Adequately evaluating the potential of managers for higher responsibilities.
—— Providing sound promotion and career opportunities for managers.
—— Filling key middle and top management positions with well-qualified persons.
—— Reducing attrition among managers at all levels.
—— Reducing attrition among capable young managers.

—— Keeping the management compensation system up-to-date and effective as a motivator.

—— Identifying objectives for management development programs.

—— Developing managers for higher level responsibilities.

—— Preventing experienced managers from growing obsolete.

—— Motivating managers to effectively develop subordinates.

—— Providing meaningful job assignments for managers throughout their career.

—— Identifying career mobility patterns for managers.

—— Maintaining a sound and flexible organization structure.

—— Anticipating organizational design changes and preparing for their manpower implications.

—— Managing the retirement pattern to help prevent replacement problems.

—— Researching the causes and solutions of serious manpower problems.

—— Integrating the manpower management programs to achieve greater overall success.

—— Obtaining top management and organizational support for manpower management programs.

—— Integrating manpower programs with overall organization objectives.

—— Measuring the labor productivity improvements of the workforce.

—— Establishing meaningful objectives of manpower management programs.

CHAPTER 3

MANPOWER PLANNING ACTION PROGRAMS

Few terms are as common in management literature as "job rotation" and it is safe to say that few are as misunderstood.
— HAROLD KOONTZ and CYRIL O'DONNELL

Ultimate success in manpower planning rests first on the quality of the action programs established to achieve manpower objectives and second on the ability of the organization to implement these programs. The programming work in manpower planning encompasses the traditional areas of personnel management. The planning approach brings the interrelationships of the various activities of personnel management into clear focus, a result that constitutes one of the major benefits of manpower planning.

The action programming work is directed both at company-wide problems and at the careers of individual managers. Mapping of strategies to achieve overall manpower goals must usually be accompanied by efforts that will assist in directing the careers of individuals. This type of career management does not involve a long-range assignment schedule for a manager; the objective, rather, is to assure that individuals are given full opportunity to demonstrate their competence and skills. Frequently this involves the development of an information system which easily identifies all managers with qualifications for vacancies in the organization, as well as attempts to provide managers, at critical periods in their careers, the work experiences important to long-range success.

The discussion in this chapter is designed to provide information on manpower planning programs used by American companies to cope with their manpower problems. The programs presented are not necessarily highly sophisticated. They are a blend of both traditional and experimental efforts and are affected by the practical attitudes of those who use them.

It is not possible to present or review all the approaches used by management to cope with the problems in the various areas covered. The bibliography provides leads to much of the source material on the subjects.

The material is organized around the conceptual relationship of the action program activities shown in Figure 3-1. The employment process is viewed as a series of events which occur during the association of the manager with the organization, an association managed by various employment process programs. In addition, a number of support programs exist to improve the effectiveness of the employment process. Manpower information, such as appraisal data, is generated and used by these employment and support programs. In addition, a specialized information base is used to produce specialized information for both support and employment process programs.

The utilization and promotion of managers are covered under the heading of mobility patterns; recruitment and selection are treated together because of their close interrelationship. Among the support activities, appraisal and management development programs are given particular attention because of their important role in management manpower planning. (Manpower forecasting and program control are the subjects of separate chapters and are, therefore, not discussed in this chapter.)

RECRUITMENT AND SELECTION

Current recruiting and selection policies and practices influence the manpower structure of an organization for many years. Some of today's hires will remain with the organization for forty years. Without a knowledge of future requirements, hiring policies tend to reflect only the current manpower structure and current manpower needs. The current situation, however, may indicate actions incompatible with future needs.

In a manpower planning program, quantitative and qualitative estimates of future requirements are combined to form the criteria which guide college recruiting. A manpower forecast can be used to set recruiting quotas for a five- or ten-year period. (The development of such a quota is outlined in Chapter 4.) The qualitative aspects of college recruiting center on the type of person to recruit. These factors may relate either to the man's management potential or to his academic training.

FIGURE 3-1

A MANPOWER MANAGEMENT FRAMEWORK

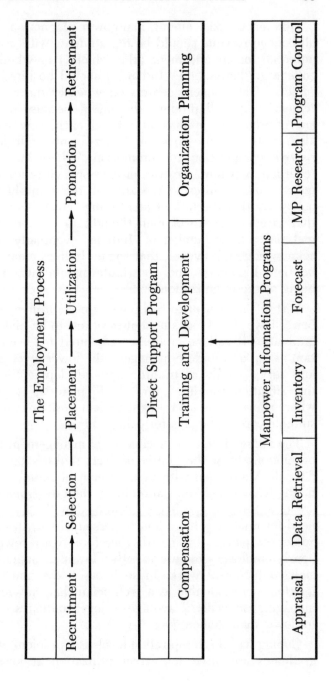

The Employment Process

Recruitment → Selection → Placement → Utilization → Promotion → Retirement

Direct Support Program

Compensation | Training and Development | Organization Planning

Manpower Information Programs

Appraisal | Data Retrieval | Inventory | Forecast | MP Research | Program Control

Differences exist among manpower planners as to whether all college recruits should be top students with apparent high potential for advancement (the "chiefs") or whether average college graduates (the "Indians") should be hired along with "chiefs." The concern centers on whether the recruitment of "chiefs" only will produce discontent because of a potential lack of promotion opportunities for all of the new hires. Concern also exists the presence of "chiefs" only will lead to disruptive competition for promotions. These two factors are regarded as potential causes of excessive early attrition among recent college hires. Advocates of the don't-hire-"Indians"-policy say that the task of identifying "chiefs" is very difficult; that in every group of men thought to be bona fide "chief" material, a large number of "Indians" eventually emerge. It is acknowledged, however, that some "Indians" may turn out to be "late bloomers" and contribute significantly to the well-being of the organization.

Part of the answer to this policy question involves the number of lower level management positions to be filled by college graduates. If college graduates are hired for eventual utilization as top and middle managers, the lower level management jobs serve mainly as training and development positions. In this situation the need for "chief" material is greater than where many of the lower management positions are considered suitable career plateaus for college hires.

The filling of first and second level management positions by promotions from the hourly or craft ranks is becoming more difficult. Many men with management potential who formerly might have joined the labor force directly from high school are now attending college. Combined with this trend is the need for relatively more hourly personnel with technical skills. Some companies are faced, therefore, with fewer qualified hourly employees for use in either lower management or specialized technical work. In such cases, the hourly employee is often more valuable as a technician than he would be as a manager, especially if average college graduates can be hired for lower management jobs.

Coping with high aspiration levels is a problem when college graduates are hired for career utilization at lower management. Some companies that hire lower quality graduates tell these men when they are hired that their managerial potential may be limited. They are told that because other college hires have demonstrated superior performance in college and on selection tests, the competition for advancement will be keen, but that demonstrated good performance will be rewarded with promotions.

A major qualitative recruiting problem relating to the background of the college graduate is the role of the liberal arts graduate in the organization. Some persons believe that the liberal arts major has greater breadth of knowledge than the graduate of a science, engineering, or business school. This breadth is regarded as especially valuable for superior performance in an increasingly complex environment. Liberal arts majors are also regarded by some as having high potential for vision and creativity.

These abilities, however, may have little room to flourish in large companies except in middle and upper management jobs. College recruiters are handicapped in hiring such persons because most of the positions they are filling require men with specific skills and training. The accountant, engineer, or financial analyst is sought because he is productive shortly after being hired. As one college recruiting official said:

> Yes, our president made a speech to the effect that we need more liberal arts majors. But we won't hire many because a manager has to pay the salary from his budget. Our managers want someone to fill a vacancy—and that someone has to know something about business or engineering.

The current high demand for engineers and science majors in part reflects a need for men with technical knowledge, and in part a desire to employ men trained to an analytical approach to problems. Companies are also increasingly interested in men with training in the mathematical, behavioral, and economic concepts important to long-run managerial success.[1] The high-

---

[1] For the view of the business educator see: Robert A. Gordon and James E. Howell, *Higher Education for Business* (New York: Columbia University Press, 1959); Frank C. Pearson, *et al., The Education of the American Businessman* (New York: McGraw-Hill Book Company, 1959); and Clinton A. Phillips, *Experience with Undergraduate Business Programs* (New Orleans: Tulane University School of Business Administration, 1964).

ly analytical approach to management initiated by schools such as Carnegie Tech, Purdue, MIT, and Tulane is being followed by other schools.[2] The graduate of schools with modern management curricula may have an undergraduate degree in engineering or science, but he is sought for long-term utilization because of his skill in analysis and logic, not only for his engineering or scientific knowledge.

As organizations increase their emphasis on sophisticated analysis in decision-making, the liberal arts major without good analytical training may find himself at an increasing disadvantage in a management career. The solution to the problem may rest in attempts by organizations to identify positions that do not require special training for successful performance. Through good supervision and on-the-job training, these men can be given the analytical background needed for long-run success. And in many instances the successful liberal arts major will contribute ideas and knowledge that the professionally trained person does not possess.[3]

Illustrations

Example 1. A long-range manpower forecast is used to determine future managerial and professional needs. College recruiting quotas are established for each year of the forecast to provide an even flow of new personnel into the firm. Previously college recruiting was tied solely to current vacancies resulting from attrition and expansion to produce a very irregular recruiting pattern. In one year the company recruited 73 men; five years later it hired only two. Recruiting officials want to eliminate their "fair weather" image on college campuses developed by their past practices. In addition, they believe the overall quality of new hires is improved because the company now is able to hire top-rated men in anticipation

---

[2] One of the most significant events in business education was the modern curriculum adopted by the Carnegie Tech School of Industrial Administration in the 1950's. The Carnegie model, with emphasis on mathematics, economics, and the behavioral sciences, provided direction for other institutions wishing to modernize their approach to business education.

[3] Management and personnel journals contain an increasing number of articles on the kind of person needed by business. Many of these articles stress the need for creativity among future managers. See, for example, "Is Business Developing the Right Kind of Manager?" Bernard J. Bienvenu, *Personnel* (May-June 1964).

of future needs. The training and development programs have benefited from the more stabilized personnel intake, and the ability of the company to absorb new personnel has risen.

Example 2. A study of technological change in production operations revealed that the technical knowledge required of new hires is changing significantly. Some engineering jobs are becoming more demanding technically and require men with advanced engineering training. On the other hand, many other jobs are becoming less technical and require men with some technical knowledge and a potential for movement into management. A de-emphasis on recruiting relatively scarce chemical engineers is one result of this analysis. Engineers with other degrees are now considered for openings formerly reserved for chemical engineers. Non-engineering graduates are used in positions of a semi-technical nature requiring only a general science and mathematics background. It was also found that some experienced hourly employees displaced by technology have the potential to occupy engineering jobs if given special training. Programs developed in conjunction with a local university now enable the company to train these displaced workers for the jobs. This in turn has relieved the demand for college-trained engineers.

Example 3. In order to improve the selection of new first level supervisors from candidates in the hourly ranks, special assessment methods are used. All persons interested in a potential move into management are sent to an assessment center where they are evaluated for three or four days by a specialty-trained assessment team composed of staff personnel experts and lower level operating managers. The candidates are given a set of psychological tests, placed in group dynamic situations, perform in management simulation exercises (e.g., in-basket, gaming), are observed in group discussions, and are interviewed by team members.

Overall results of the program have been outstanding, according to the firm. A significant drop in the number of men who are promoted but subsequently fail as first level supervisors is the major benefit. In addition, the increased understanding by aspirants for supervision of the duties and problems of a manager causes some to decide they do not want to be in management. Better understanding of their own duties as managers by the lower level managers serving as assessment team members and improved understanding of the needs of employees are also reported as benefits of the program. Statistical validation of the various assessment devices has been made to improve the means used and to shorten the assessment period.

A somewhat similar program is used in another company to assess the potential of middle managers for higher level jobs. The activities to which these managers are exposed are of a higher managerial level. The results of the assessments are used by corporate staff manpower planners, with performance and potential appraisal data, to plan future assignments.

PLACEMENT POLICIES

Early job assignments of managers have a significant influence on their career development. If the assignment requires a college graduate to assume responsibility and perform to the extent of his abilities, attitudes and habits are formed which may help the individual throughout his career. Such assignments may also convince a new employee that the performance expectations of the organization require sacrifices that he does not wish to make. The new employee discovers what he can expect from the organization and the organization is able to determine what it can expect from its new talent.

These factors have caused many companies to abandon initial placement methods that involved rotating a new hire through several departments. The rotating programs frequently revealed little about the abilities of the new hire because few, if any, significant tasks were assigned to him. Careful placement of new hires into positions which utilize their talents and provide a sense of accomplishment help to reduce high early turnover rates. Capable and ambitious college graduates quickly become dissatisfied with assignments that require little thought or effort. In addition, such assignments are expensive when salary costs are equated with the returns to the organization.

Initial placement in positions which provide useful experience for future career assignments ideally involves: learning to assume responsibility; the development of initiative; and learning how to make and live with decisions that may result in mistakes.

Illustrations

Example 1. Examination of the qualifications of existing managers for promotion into middle and top management revealed deficiencies in their breadth of knowledge of overall company operations. New vacancies at these levels require this knowledge. This trend is expected to continue. Revisions in placement programs for new hires were made to avoid this situation in the future.

New hires are frequently assigned to the computer operation to acquire a broad overview of the company operations and its information systems. Industrial engineering is another area used for career development purposes. The company wants future staff managers to understand manufacturing operations before engaging in finance, marketing, or accounting activities. Industrial engineering placement provides broader manufacturing exposure than a first line supervisor's job, and the company is able to utilize non-engineering graduates in some jobs in this department.

Budget restraints may prevent a department considered good for initial placement from hiring additional manpower. To meet this problem, the personnel department is budgeted to employ several new college hires for initial placement purposes. Personnel pays for the new hire from its budget and loans the man to another activity. After several months of this arrangement, personnel will withdraw the man unless the borrowing department picks the man up on its own budget. Experience shows that internal budget adjustments may sometimes be made by the borrowing department in order not to lose the services of an individual. Impetus for this program arose when the company was forced to decline the opportunity to acquire another company because of lack of manpower to staff the proposed subsidiary. Part of the current college recruiting and placement activity is designed to provide long-run management depth to permit future growth via acquisitions.

Example 2. The initial long-range manpower forecast showed a need for many college graduates to replace retiring executives. A study made to identify positions in the forecast that could be staffed by non-college men revealed that 70 positions currently filled by college graduates did not require college education. For planning purposes, it was assumed that half of the men in these positions were improperly placed, but that half of them were unqualified for more demanding work. Further investigation revealed that none of the 70 men possessed advancement potential. Young men in this group with only a few years of service were told their futures were limited and to seek new employment elsewhere. Upcoming retirements solved several of the other assignment problems. The remaining men were retained but "dead-ended" with respect to promotion unless an amazing improvement was made in their performance. Steps were taken to avoid a repetition of the situation through gradual elimination of many of the jobs and more careful placement work.

None of the men affected were told about the study. The company is very reluctant to separate salaried personnel with more than a few years of service. Because of this attitude, a manager involved in the analysis privately conceded that the company would probably always be plagued by the situation.[4]

Example 3. College hires are assigned to highly regarded managers in positions that require intelligence and hard work. A college recruiting coordinator holds bimonthly meetings with the men individually and as a group to discuss their assignments, company operations, and their progress and development. Bimonthly group meetings are also held with the supervisors to discuss the progress of the men, to evaluate the assignments given them, and to provide the supervisors with insights and ideas for the development of young men. This program lasts a year. At the end of the year the men are evaluated to determine if they should continue to be employed. A

---

[4] This example apparently is not an isolated one. Harry Levinson, head of the industrial mental health division of the Menninger Foundation, reports of similar incidents of organizations unwilling to release managers. Levinson calls this inability of managers to recognize the meaning of their own feelings and their unwillingness to recognize their own displeasure and anger with subordinates, "management by guilt." In the company example cited, the apparently "kind" approach may be more of a sop to management's conscience than objectivity and fairness to the employee. See Harry Levinson, *Emotional Health in the World of Work* (New York: Harper & Row, 1964).

key objective is to provide control over initial assignments to insure they are meaningful to career growth. In addition, the assignments enable the organization to gain meaningful evaluation information on the new employees.

MOBILITY PATTERNS

Programs designed to provide a pattern to the mobility of management manpower result from quantitative and qualitative manpower objectives. In the mobility pattern context the definition of manpower planning is particularly significant. Having managers properly placed in the organization at a given point in time is seen in terms of both future and past utilization.

Mobility pattern programs relate to broad organizational manpower goals and to individual manager career patterns. A program to provide control over the rate of upward mobility of managers may be aimed at accelerating development to insure that an adequate number of men will be available for future middle and top management positions, or its objective may be to meet problems anticipated because of an impending slowdown in the advancement rate. In such a situation, increased lateral transfers may be made when upward moves are limited. The transfers help provide needed stimulation to the manager by providing new job environments that otherwise might be lacking. The need to examine the salary ranges for particular job levels is also important in this situation to insure that this motivational instrument is properly related to the mobility program.

Another mobility program is related to the development of specific managerial skills through lateral transfers of managers into specialized departments (e.g., financial planning skills). These programs are closely involved with the management's development efforts discussed below. The concern is with designing cross-training efforts at various levels in light of future needs of the organization and of the demands these needs will place on managers.

A third mobility program involves the designing of preferred career patterns for potential top and middle managers. Here the planner identifies the type of experience that appears especially valuable in a successful managerial career. Knowing when this experience is best gained and how it relates to previous experiences is involved. A number of career paths may be developed for various types of managers. The planner determines, for example, the kinds of experience that are most beneficial to engineers who may move into middle and top engineering management jobs. This does not mean that every engineer must be assigned design engineering work early in his career. It may mean, however, that at some time within the first ten years of employment, every engineer with higher management potential may expect to be given experience as a group project manager or leader. Such a program precludes the possibility of an engineer's reaching a significant management level only through individual work assignments or as a member of a project group. The same kind of reasoning is used in identifying career patterns in other career fields. (A list of considerations that may provide guidance to the design of career mobility patterns is contained in the appendix to this chapter.)

Efforts to implement mobility pattern programs are frequently enhanced through an overall manpower planning program. The inventory of current manpower resources and identification of future requirements may cause resisting departments to become more aware of their overall organizational manpower problems and needs. When this happens, cross-departmental transfers and promotions tend to become easier to effect. Along with preparing men for future responsibilities more intelligently, mobility programs that cut across the entire organization permit ability and performance to be rewarded more consistently throughout the organization. When transfers and promotions between organizational units are artificially impeded, rapid advancements may occur in one department for men of a given age, level, and talent, while comparable men in another department are stymied in their careers.

In addition to planned progression rates and interdepartmental mobility, greater acceptance of outsiders for positions that cannot be filled internally may result from mobility programs. As one executive said, "Because we are doing a better job of creating opportunities for men throughout the organization, we have fewer negative reactions when we are forced to hire an experienced man from the outside."

Illustrations

Example 1. When a vacancy occurs, the manpower planner notifies supervisors throughout the company and requests names of men who might qualify for the position. These names are sent to the supervisor in whose unit the vacancy exists, with a data summary of the individuals. The supervisor will screen these records and then interview the best prospects. He also retains freedom to promote from his own organization under this procedure. Top management supports the promotion system by salary increases to managers whose subordinates receive promotions to positions in other departments. (Managers who attempt to export weak personnel are given an effective "correction" treatment by the informal organization.) The procedure improves manpower utilization throughout the organization by providing a larger manpower pool from which to fill vacancies. In addition, turnover among the best young men is reduced, better and more rapid development takes place, and managers throughout the organization are more aware of their responsibilities in the selection, development, and promotion of subordinates.

Example 2. Concern over a lack of potential top management replacements and the need to recruit such men from outside resulted in a study of the middle management structure and of the promotion paths to top management. It was found that several key positions on the path were occupied by capable but non-promotable men in their early fifties. As a result, some men in their late thirties and early forties with top management potential were blocked in their career paths. To help solve the problem, a younger man is moved into the key position. The previous position holder is made an "assistant to" the younger man to help train and develop the new incumbent. "Task force" assignments are also given the older man, but his primary duty is rapid development of the younger man for periods up to three years. When the younger man is assigned another job (usually a pre-determined vacancy resulting from a retirement or a promotion) the senior man resumes his former position.

Because of the potential human conflict problems in this procedure, the company selects men for such moves with great care. Top management believes, however, that a senior middle manager has a responsibility to help develop capable future top managers. It also believes that the younger man must have the full responsibility and pressure of a position to be properly tested and developed. A relatively small upper middle management structure prevents the company from opening up the development positions by transferring the senior manager to a new assignment.

Example 3. A lack of experienced men for positions as plant managers and assistant plant managers resulted in the design of a career promotion pattern that would produce future needed talent. New engineers with MBA degrees are initially assigned staff jobs in areas such as quality control, systems management, budgeting, and operations research. Good performers are then given a line assignment as manufacturing foremen or minor department heads. Success in these jobs indicates long-range potential in either line or staff work, although the company expects to utilize the men primarily in a line capacity. The company wants to provide its future top line managers with lower level manufacturing experience as well as staff work. In the past, top quality men who began their careers in staff jobs did not receive lower line experience. They thus were often not considered for positions at the plant manager level, which is a key position for future top managers.

RETIREMENT

The proper spacing of normal and early retirements is helpful to a company with either manpower shortages or special development problems for younger manpower. Early retirements help space out periods of higher than average retirements that result from an uneven age distribution. They also help trigger a series of promotions considered desirable for future staffing reasons. In other cases, utilization of personnel beyond the normal retirement age is an important means of "buying time" for the development of younger manpower.

Illustration

Example. In order to encourage early retirements to help level out several years of impending peak retirements, early retirement benefits were greatly liberalized. These revisions induced several executives to retire. Where the company wished to retire a number of other managers early because they occupied strategic positions from a management development standpoint, individual financial arrangements were made because of special financial problems of some managers. A few managers who declined to retire early were eventually told to either retire or resign. The company was reluctant to adopt this policy, but top management was convinced that the long-range manpower situation required unusual action. It believed the extra expense of the early retirement provisions was more than justified by the long-run returns of an adequate future manpower structure.

COMPENSATION PROGRAMS

Although in most companies wages and salaries are administered by staff specialists using well-established procedures, compensation rates require attention in manpower planning. In Chapter 7, the interrelationships of the manpower forecast, profit plan, and the future wage bill are discussed. In wage and salary administration terms, the thrust of the Chapter 7 discussion is the establishment of long-range criteria for control over the total wage bill. This manpower forecasting aspect of manpower planning requires the wage and salary administrator to evaluate the trend in his programs, to estimate future total wage costs accurately, and to program future wage and benefit costs over a period of time in order to help the organization attain labor productivity objectives.

The relationship of starting wages to the existing wage structure, and the motivational aspects of wages and benefits, also require careful attention. Control over total wage costs may result in a wage program of modest wage increases for experienced personnel, but regular large increases in starting salaries for new engineers and managers. The closing of the differential between new and experienced manpower tends to increase the voluntary termination rate of experienced men who come to believe their salary prospects are poor with their present employers but that they can command a higher salary with another company. A manpower planning approach to wage and salary administration includes consideration of the replacement cost of experienced manpower.

Another manpower planning aspect of wage and salary administration is the relationship of the performance appraisal program to salary increases. An engineer in a company with an elaborate performance evaluation system summed up the attitude of many of his colleagues by saying, "I look at what happens to my paycheck to figure out what my evaluation really means."

At another company, a young manager said, "When I came with this company I figured out what I should be earning each of my first three years. I got a raise last week that keeps me on schedule. But I would have quit in three more weeks if the raise hadn't come along. It is hard to figure the company because my boss told me six months ago that I had been given a very good performance rating. Yet he didn't put me in for a raise until just recently."

These two remarks emphasize the need to develop a clearly understood relationship between performance appraisal and salary administration — either they are related or they are not related. Arguments can be, and have been, developed for each approach. The important consideration is that the wage and salary program shall be integrated with the total motivational and reward system of the organization. This requires the identification of the criteria which influence the wage and salary program from an overall manpower planning point of view.

Information on the salary performance of an individual is useful in interpreting his past performance as a manager. Useful information on the salary history of managers that can be recorded for future interpretation includes:

a. The date and amount of each salary increase.
b. The percentage increase of each raise over the previous salary.
c. The reason for the salary increase:
    — merit increase.
    — general salary adjustment.
    — promotion increase.
d. The position of the mid-year (or year-end) salary in the salary classification range.
e. The percentage salary increase during the past year versus the average increase for all managers in the same salary classification.

This type of information helps the manpower planner to determine the reasons for past salary progress and the per-

formance significance of a salary increase. The ability to compare the performance of an individual against all other managers in the same wage classification is especially valuable in
studying salary progress and overall performance. Men consistently below the mid-range of a salary classification, for
example, are usually those who have had above-average promotion progress. Usually they have lacked time in each salary
group to have moved above the mid-range through the general
salary adjustments given the entire managerial group.

Illustrations

Example 1. The study of labor productivity data for manpower forecasting purposes also provides useful information
for union wage negotiations. Wage increase effects on profits
are now better understood and the company attempts to bar-
gain in anticipation of labor productivity gains. The inclusion
of fringe benefit costs in the productivity analysis causes plant
managers to become more concerned about fringe benefit
bargaining, whereas in the past, these managers were almost
exclusively concerned with direct hourly wage increases. The
company is also more confident in its ability to negotiate wage
increases in return for freedom in job transfers and temporary
worker reassignments because of the productivity data. Greater
freedom in these two areas is expected to further increase
labor productivity.

Example 2. The introduction of electronic data processing
equipment created wage and job classification problems for
displaced workers. The policy developed to facilitate transfers
of these workers was unsatisfactory for computer programmers
who were surplused when the EDP system became fully operational. New wage policies were established to accommodate
the job transfer of programmers. Still later, a group of engineers
became surplus and another policy was developed for their
reassignment. These relocations revealed a need for broader
wage policies tied to long-range manpower needs. Greater
flexibility in wage administration became an objective to eliminate the need for top management's approval and probable
delay on wage matters after each worker dislocation. An attempt to forecast future technological and organizational
changes was included. The wage and salary administrator now

works closely with the organization planner. As the organization planner attempts to develop consistency in the organization structure, long-range wage and salary considerations are given serious consideration. This effort now results in fewer new positions which require modification or exception from the overall salary structure.

MANAGEMENT DEVELOPMENT PROGRAMS

The major role of management development activities in manpower planning and management is emphasized by the wealth of information published on this subject. The shape and form of the programs are varied and undergo constant change as new managerial manpower needs are revealed. The key relationship of manpower planning to traditional management development work is the determination of objectives for management development. Manpower forecasting and goal-setting activities of manpower planning facilitate determination of development objectives.

Manpower planning not only helps determine future manpower needs, but also the capability of the existing stock of manpower, and the time period in which to prepare men for future responsibilities. This information, with estimates of the future organization design and qualitative manpower requirements, provides guidance to the management development expert in his work. Unfortunately, many management development programs in American industry lack such clear-cut, meaningful objectives.

But having objectives for the activity still does not produce instant managers. Formalized classroom work, job rotations, and special coaching will not transform weak managers into strong managers — at least not with any degree of regularity. This philosophy is implicit in manpower planning: management development begins the first day a manager reports to work and ends the day of his retirement.

The evidence of the behavioral scientists with respect to human development, learning, thinking, and problem-solving clearly indicates that success in the development of managers must be primarily rooted in the job of the manager and in his general environment. This does not mean that special seminars, conferences, and workshops are unimportant or lack value as means of training — especially for the development of specific skills or techniques. Such endeavors are primarily useful to fill the gaps in the learning that occurs on the job.

Meaningful job assignments as part of a generalized plan of development, in addition to providing exposure to important problem situations and particularized operational environments, should meet several other criteria. Most important is that the assignment be of sufficient length for the manager to become significant in the definition of the job. A short tour in a special job rotation assignment does not enable the manager to imprint his style, ability, and personality on that job. As a result, the manager is unable to learn adequately from the situation and the company is unable to evaluate his performance properly.

Short tours in positions also tend to force the manager to devote much of his time to learning (but usually not mastering) the basic elements of a job without enough time to make improvements in it. When the highly talented person is considered as an agent of change in an organization that person must have opportunity to make changes, changes that should be in more than minor detailed items. They should be of the type that enables the organization to adjust to its changing operational environment.

Another factor in management development job assignments is the need to provide a manager with a sure grasp of the details of certain jobs. Success in higher management positions frequently rests on the ability of the manager to understand and interpret data. Knowledge of reference points, and the ability to cut through the irrevelant, are enhanced by understanding the significance of particular key bits of information. In addition, knowledge of details enables a manager to maintain more effective control of his operations. This ability to control affects his current performance and ultimate promotability to higher level responsibilities.

In developing men for advancement, providing a man with a home department that serves as a major specialty area is helpful. During the early years of his career, assignments should enable him to learn many of the operating problems and important details of an organization operation. Broadening experience needed for higher management can be gained at the middle management level in positions throughout the organization. This approach also enables the organization to utilize middle managers who fail to demonstrate higher level potential in a field of specialization. It helps to avoid the problem of effective utilization of managers who lack the necessary experience to manage in specialized fields. These facts do not imply that young lower level managers should spend long periods in one job assignment. What is suggested is that the men remain in a special field of activity long enough to fully understand its many dimensions. Then, should they be transferred out of the activity for several years, they can return at a higher level of responsibility with basic knowledge for successful performance.

Job rotation and transfer, important as they are to the development process, must be tempered by the recognition that mere exposure to a variety of jobs does not insure that the desired learning and development are occurring. In the next section, the discussion of promotion policies emphasizes the importance of identifying the promotion paths that lead to higher level responsibilities. These paths frequently require exposure to a variety of situations that cut across department lines. In the development of these paths, however, the management development requirements should be given special attention.

Another criterion in management development programs, and one that is frequently overlooked, is the need to provide reinforcers for managers in their responsibilities of developing the abilities of subordinates. Performance appraisal programs frequently give little or no attention to the managers' development efforts. Salary merit increases often are made with the idea that good management development work is reflected in better group performance and thus is implicitly recognized. Unfortunately, the manager devoting time and energy to development work may not see this relationship. The environment for management development thus should support the trainer as well as the trainee.

Another frequently neglected, but important, aspect of management development is evaluation of returns on the development investment made in managers. This neglect stems mainly from the difficulties of measuring the results of training and development and of matching returns with costs.

Although full treatment of this subject is not possible here, the importance of attempting to determine the results of development efforts in order to utilize development monies more wisely should be a readily acceptable idea. This recognition leads to the need for objectives in management development, the establishment of indices to show whether the objectives are being achieved, and a suitable time frame for use in measuring returns. In addition, a subjective determination of the value of various objectives should be made to evaluate actual and potential development costs.

For example, just how important to the organization is a 20 per cent improvement in the planning skills of middle managers? Is it worth $500, $5,000, or $50,000? The answer to such a question can perhaps only be learned through experiment. Some means of measuring planning ability must be found and of measuring the impact of planning on the manager's productivity. The use of a control group and an experimental development group may lead to some of the answers. Certainly pilot-program efforts in this area appear desirable before an organization-wide evaluation project is undertaken.

Another investment aspect of management development centers on which individuals to select for major development attention. Development programs may have different payoff periods; it is important to select men with high return potential for expensive, long-term programs. Training in human relations and leadership, for example, may be a long-term effort with a long-run payoff, but only minor, immediately visible results. In other cases, training in budgeting, cost analysis, or computer uses may produce some highly visible results rather quickly.

The economic answer to the selection problem is to choose subjects for major development attention who appear to have the potential to yield the highest returns. Managers highly rated on past and present performance and potential appraisal often qualify on this criterion. But which of the average and below-average performers should receive major attention? The use of testing instruments, recommendations by superiors, and special assessment centers may help provide the answer. Another method is to allow all managers to participate in some training and development work, then to identify for major attention those managers who respond most favorably to the programs. Under this method, the organization is able continually to upgrade the entire managerial workforce, and every manager has several opportunities to qualify for special attention. At the same time, the increase in the development investment per individual is controlled so that it is concentrated on men who demonstrate that they yield a good return.

Such an approach requires an information system which stores data on the development attention given managers. It records information on seminars, conferences, summer institutes, and their special work assignments. Job performance and potential evaluations can be related to these data to help the organization improve its planning and management of management development.

Finally, it is important to remember always that the experience a manager gains on the job is part of the firm's investment in him. An opportunity cost situation exists in every work assignment. The comparative values of giving one man an opportunity to gain certain experience, with the loss resulting from not giving someone else that experience, or of not giving that man some other kind of experience must be weighed. Attempts should be made to determine both the short- and long-term benefits of the experience to the organization and to the manager. Thinking of these assignment opportunity costs, in part at least, as investments that yield future returns helps to improve placement and development decisions.

Illustrations

Example 1. Requests from younger managers for assignment to a particular company location led to an investigation that revealed that the manager in charge is an exceptional developer of young men and that his reputation had circulated informally among lower level managers. The manager takes special pride in his development efforts and follows the career patterns of many former subordinates. The operation itself is ideal for development because it is a scaled-down model of activities in larger cities. This finding led to identification of other managers with ability to develop subordinates and of other good training locations. The company assigns young men with high potential either to a good developer of managers or to a good training location. Important to the success of the program are salary incentives for managers who do a good job in management development activities.

Example 2. Overstaffing has resulted in excessive job specialization for many managers. Manpower forecasts indicate a reduction in the total management group, even though the company expects to grow. Programs to increase job responsibility for managers are now used to utilize and develop their talents. As vacancies occur, jobs are eliminated, and position responsibilities are reassigned. Job responsibilities which are too narrow, the company believes, are the costly penalty of overstaffing because they restrict the development of managers.

Example 3. This company is concerned with using its management training dollars in the best manner possible. When a specialized training program is needed, the firm tries to use its own personnel as trainers in order to reinforce general training material with company policies and practices. When an employee attends an outside program or summer seminar, he appraises its quality, the type of persons who benefit by attendance, and its long-range value. Reports now exist on a thousand such training programs. Only organizations and colleges with a record of sponsoring programs of value to the company are used in the training and development program.

ORGANIZATION PLANNING PROGRAMS

One of the most difficult activities in manpower planning is assisting the organization structure to adjust to new demands upon it. Changes in objectives, operations, and personnel lead to a number of organizational realignments. Frequently these changes arise to solve short-run problems and are not the result of planning for longer-run requirements. To help cope with this situation, organization planning groups advise departments on organization changes and make recommendations on proposed changes to higher management.

The role of the manpower planner in these activities is

important because managerial manpower governs the success or failure of an organization design. Furthermore, it is undesirable to design organizations without giving thought to staffing requirements.

These considerations stipulate that the manpower planner give serious attention to organization planning matters. He should ask whether the current organization design best services the broad objectives of the company. In reviewing plans for new organizational relationships, he should inquire whether these plans will make the best use of existing and future managerial talents. When analyzing the quality of current manpower, he should also ask if new organization designs would help solve some of the company's manpower problems. In general he should be conscious of the interrelationships between manpower planning and organization planning and he must coordinate closely with company organization planners. If such persons do not exist, he should assume some of the responsibilities for organization planning in order to increase the effectiveness of the manpower planning effort.[5]

A fundamental organization planning task of the manpower planner is to identify the key management positions at various levels throughout the company. These "first team" positions should be filled by high quality manpower. The planner should know which men are top performers and which positions require top talent. He should work with departments to see that "first team" men are filling "first team" jobs to enable the organization to have "the right man, in the right job, at the right time."

Illustrations

Example 1. An ideal long-range organization chart is developed on the basis of product line activities the company anticipates for five years into the future. Basic organization structure changes are made with this design in mind, and

---

[5] In Chapter 4, some of the organization planning considerations involved in estimating staffing requirements of the future management structure are discussed. For an interesting example of organization planning see Kilburn LeCompte, "Organizational Structures in Transition," in *Some Theories of Organization*, Albert Rubenstein and Chadwick Haberstroh (eds.) (Rev. ed.) (Homewood, Illinois: Dorsey Press, 1966).

proposals incompatible with the long-range structure are modified. No attempt is made to achieve the ideal structure immediately. The current structure is gradually modified as opportunities arise and as personnel changes. Responsibility for the future organization rests with an executive assistant to the chief operating officer.

Example 2. A long-range manpower forecast revealed that future marketing manpower needs would totally absorb all the manpower the company could economically tolerate. To help reduce this manpower requirement, the manpower planning group assisted in an organization planning study. The result was a consolidation of many field marketing management jobs, which led to an actual short-run reduction of marketing manpower requirements. Without the planning effort it is believed that marketing would have increased its manpower to a level that would have greatly complicated any reorganization attempts.

Example 3. The need for coordination of organization and manpower planning is clearly demonstrated in this rapidly growing company. Here the manpower planner and the organization planner report through separate channels to top management and are not officially coordinated. The manpower planner said requests for information on future organization growth were met with responses such as "We're too busy trying to straighten out the operating divisions to give time to the future organization." Long-range financial objectives rest heavily on expansion of international operations. This growth will require the formation of new corporate level departments and many new reporting relationships. Because he can not work with the organization planner, the manpower planner is handicapped in his development of manpower forecasts. This retards recruitment and development efforts for long-range needs at a time when current growth is straining available managerial resources.

APPRAISAL PROGRAMS

Qualitative information on the current performance of managers and on their future potential is needed in planning the staffing of the future management structure. This area of manpower management is discussed intensively in the literature, and in management seminars. The attention given appraisal methods has not solved the problem of how to obtain useful and accurate information.[6]

The root of many appraisal problems is the search for objectivity while relying on subjective opinions of performance. This is especially true of evaluations of future potential because variables influencing future success may not be present, or at least significant, in the current job assignment.

One recent approach to the problem is to establish performance goals against which the manager is evaluated. This method is supposed to build objectivity into the appraisal process, but it may provide little information on the promotion potential of the manager. The determination of "realistic" goals is a subjective agreement between the supervisor and his subordinate.

Concern with subjectivity in evaluations is important, although it can be overemphasized. It is impossible for most appraisers to suspend their subjective opinions completely, and in many instances this subjective judgment may be the most important information that can be gained from an appraisal process. What is required is to train managers in the art of distinguishing between information which is based on subjective opinion and that which is based on objective performance results. In the final analysis, successful past performance may still be the best single indicator of future success.

Early Identification Systems

Directly linked to appraisal programs are attempts to identify the long-range potential of younger managers. The objective of these early identification programs is information on high quality manpower that will improve with good utilization.

Some of the early identification techniques are the result of efforts by psychologists. The use of tests to identify potential has been explored in depth at Standard Oil of New Jersey,[7]

---

[6] For a critical review of the state of the art of performance appraisal, see George S. Odiorne, *Personnel Policy: Issues and Practices*, Chapter 13, "What's Wrong with Appraisal Systems?" (Columbus, Ohio: Charles E. Merrill Books, 1963).

[7] Harry Laurent, "The Identification of Management Potential." Paper presented before the Division of Industrial Psychology, American Psychological Association, September 5, 1962 St. Louis, Missouri.

where the researchers express confidence in their methods as a means of identifying managerial talents before a man has been given responsibilities requiring the use of these talents. Operating companies of AT&T are using both depth interviews and psychological tests to gain insights on the career potential of young men.[8]

In general, however, most early identification efforts rely on the opinions of supervisors of the man being appraised. When early identification information is gained in this manner, it is desirable that the person identified as having very high potential be required to demonstrate this potential to another manager. Although the "halo" effect is not eliminated by such a procedure, qualities of special appeal to one manager do not thus, in themselves, carry a man into higher level responsibilities.

Illustrations

Example 1. Dissatisfaction with information on current and potential performance needed for placement planning led to the establishment of two special staff positions. The staff specialist was assigned the responsibility of assisting managers throughout the organization in their evaluation of subordinates by standarized criteria. Early results of the program indicate an improvement in the potential ratings, but higher quality results are still being sought.

Example 2. Need for information on the potential top managers required for long-range manpower planning resulted in the creation of an early identification system. Previously information on top management potential had been sought only on middle managers, for it had been believed that several years of company work experience were needed before an identification of top management potential could be made. The company also wished to avoid creating "halos" around talented young managers. The new system resulted in the addition of Group 4 to the following categories related to management potential:

---

[8] Frederick R. Kappel, "From the World of College to the World of Work," *Bell Telephone Magazine* (Spring 1962).

Group 1. Upper middle management men with potential for top management.

Group 2. Middle management men with potential for top management.

Group 3. Middle management men regarded as promotable but not included in Group 1 or 2.

Group 4. Lower management men qualified for very substantial advancement.

In addition to gathering these data, the company now seeks the reasons men with high potential leave the company. An exit interview is given each man when he leaves. He is contacted a year later to learn whether his new position has met his expectations and how he now regards his association with his former company.

Example 3. Each top manager independently rates all managers in the organization with respect to their promotability. Lower unit managers without college degrees are not included in this appraisal. The following rating system is used:

10 Poor Performance — Demotable.

20 Average Performance — Not Promotable.

30 Promotable One Level.

40 Promotable Two Levels.

50 Immediately Promotion One Level and Promotable Two Levels within five years.

NR No Rating due to lack of adequate information.

The second digit in each number is used to indicate the year when the man is estimated to be promotable. Thus a 32 rating indicates promotable one level in two years; a 30 indicates immediately promotable one level; and, a 42 indicates promotable one level in two years and another level later.

The ratings are collected by the manpower planner and recorded on visual aids for a conference of the top managers who made the ratings. The company president, who presides at this meeting, calls on different managers to explain their ratings, first on those who submitted very high or low ratings, to provide emphasis in the discussion of rating differences. The manager who submitted the highest rating on a man, for example, might begin the discussion. He would be followed by the manager who submitted the lowest rating on that individual. The manager whose department contains the person being evaluated comments last. The discussion of each individual results in a final potential-rating for each manager.

This activity requires at least two full days of deliberation for approximately 250 managers. The method is considered to be superior to written reports because it emphasizes debate and discussion. In addition, higher management becomes aware of the performance of men throughout the organization at all levels. Department heads must know their department manpower in order to discuss their personnel intelligently. Special weaknesses of men are revealed through the discussion. Managers learn how other department heads view individuals in their departments and thus gain insight into interdepartmental relationships. Also significant is the opportunity of department heads to learn of capable persons in other departments who might be useful additions to their own departments when a suitable vacancy occurs, which is helpful in interdepartmental transfers and overall management development.

INFORMATION RETRIEVAL SYSTEMS

Manpower planning activities involve the analysis of a wide variety of data. Information on labor productivity, the age and education of managers, the number of men considered promotable, language skills and work experience of managers, and promotion progression rates are examples of the data studied in manpower planning. The design of an information retrieval system which provides desired information is therefore important. Often the planning effort will require information that does not exist currently or exists in a form which is not conveniently usable. The new system should meet both current and forseeable needs.

Computer retrieval systems are used in these efforts to identify and retrieve personnel history information on individual managers. Human retrieval of this information is often very slow, costly, and perhaps impossible. But computer systems can also be very costly; they can also be slow if only a small amount of information is desired and access to the computer is limited.

Some of the information that companies store on tape in information retrieval systems includes the following:

Date of Birth
Date of Employment (Company, Division, etc.)
Marital Status

Dependents
Education
Military Service
Work Experience (outside company)
Job Assignments (inside company)
Management Development Attention
Performance Ratings
Potential Ratings
Salary History
Promotion Progression
Future Work Preferences
Travel Attitudes and Preferences
Special Professional Qualifications
Language Skills
Experience in Foreign Countries
Professional Associations
Publications
Civic Associations

The amount of information stored on previous job assignments and professional qualifications varies considerably by company. Organizations that employ large numbers of engineers and scientists with highly specialized skills (e.g., aerospace companies) tend to store large amounts of data on past assignments and current skills to enable them to identify personnel with unique qualifications for specialized project work.

The information retrieval system used for manpower planning may involve two or three sub-systems. A computer system may be used to develop manpower tables and to search many individual personnel records rapidly. A manual system may be used to monitor the career progression of individual managers. A third system that provides information for productivity studies might be closely related to the company's financial information system.

As understanding of the information needs of the organization increases, the ability of the manpower planner to use the computer will increase. The information systems used should be evaluated regularly to determine their adequacy and in order to design improvements.

Illustrations

Example 1. An early manpower planning activity was the development of a computerized information system to handle manpower data. Shortly after the system became operational (using tape storage of data) the magnitude of the tape updating task and constant need for new and different information caused the company to abandon the entire system. This decision was made because labor and computer costs were considered greater than the benefits received from the system. The manpower planners then determined the information of actual significance in manpower management before returning to a computer system. It was felt that the original system stored more data than were needed for high-speed processing.

Example 2. A computer manpower information retrieval system searches for qualified personnel when vacancies arise. To staff its domestic and foreign activities, the company must identify men with technical ability, proper experience, language skills, and job interest. The company tries to identify all men who meet vacancy criteria by using the system before making a selection.

Example 3. Manpower planning is a responsibility of operating divisions, with a corporate manpower planner to provide advice and guidance. A concern of the corporate level planner is the design and maintenance of the information system used by the units. The system must assist in the making of local manpower decisions, and it must furnish information requested by top corporate management on short notice. The use of high-speed computer equipment for the task proved disappointing. The major computer problem centered on an inability to retrieve a limited set of key data on very short notice. Manpower planners in the corporation are encouraged to maintain information in a form which meets the following three tests:

1. Is the information easily portable? This criterion exists because the information is used for plant, division, and corporate level discussions of manpower.

2. Are the data available for use on short notice? Here the concern is with updating records quickly to provide management with current data.

3. Once available, is the information adequate to assist in making intelligent manpower decisions? This factor involves the possibility that too much information might be generated, in addition to a potential lack of data.

To achieve these objectives, looseleaf binders with current

status sheets on all managers are used. This system permits quick reproduction of information on office copying machines as well as easy movement of the data. The status sheet design is a major element in this system and requires constant attention so that it meets current information needs.

INVENTORY PROGRAMS

Inventory programs are a key element in manpower planning because they reveal the current manpower capabilities of the organization. This information serves as the base point for manpower forecasts and for the development of manpower plans.

Inventory efforts may range from a detailed analysis of job duties and position requirements to summaries of the numbers of managers at various organization levels by age and advancement potential. The inventory should enable the analyst to determine the existing manpower by significant categories (e.g., function, experience, training, age, performance quality, etc.), where it is being utilized, and how it is being utilized. These data can be integrated into matrices for analytical purposes. To be effective and economic, the inventory effort should be coordinated with the data retrieval systems and performance and potential appraisal programs.

Designing inventory programs is a straight-forward task. The analyst first determines the type of information he should examine on a regular basis and the information that is available in the organization. He may develop special forms and data collection procedures for the actual inventory. The value of the exercise, however, lies in analysis of data once they are obtained. The discussion of inventory programs in this chapter is confined to descriptive material on the inventory. Chapter 4 is devoted to a demonstration of how inventory data on a large group of managers can be combined with a manpower forecast to reveal recruiting, management development, and promotion needs.

Perhaps the most typical inventory exercise is that which requires managers to indicate the persons who are considered "back-up" personnel should a vacancy arise in a position. This information is frequently combined with information on the age, performance quality, and promotion potential of managers and placed on manpower planning organization charts. The organization chart can be supported by summary forms which contain information on manpower by organizational units and functional activities that cut across organizational lines. The combined data provide operating managers and top management with an easily understood view of their current manpower situation. Because the data frequently reveal manpower deficiencies, they may act as a strong stimulus to operating management to improve or to change their manpower utilization.

Another inventory activity involves collecting and analyzing information on relatively large numbers of managers by locations, skills, experience, and potential. For example, an inventory may reveal that only five per cent of the managers in an organization have a working familiarity with computers and that they are concentrated at lower levels or in one or two operating units. This may be regarded as too low a percentage in light of management methods and techniques likely to be used in the future. The implications of this evaluation would be reflected in recruitment, selection, placement, and utilization decisions.

An important use of inventory data is for comparative analysis studies of manpower on a time series basis. Observing the changes in the number of men rated promotable over time may provide insights into the effectiveness of recruitment and development activities. Few companies currently maintain this type of historical information but a well-developed inventory program can provide it at very little cost. Comparative studies, however, require manpower managers to adopt a research attitude towards their work. This is something that has been lacking for too long in the manpower area.

Of special concern to some organizations are inventory data that are collected on managers who are regarded as being especially significant to the future prosperity of the firm. These efforts are important because of the "blue chip" nature of the manpower and the awareness that a relatively small set of top grade managers can make a significant difference in the well-being of the organization. The managers covered in such an inventory are generally those who are most likely to occupy major positions of responsibility at the end of a five- or ten-year period. Individual career planning programs involving carefully chosen assignments and special development work for these men result from the analysis of these inventory data.

Several criteria should govern the manpower inventory program. The first criterion is that the inventory should provide a clear and accurate picture of current manpower resources. The specific information that achieves this objective will vary with each organization and will gradually change over time.

Secondly, the inventory should assist the planner in making decisions affecting future activities in the employment process. This means that the inventory should be integrated with manpower forecast data.

Thirdly, the inventory should prove useful for analytical studies. Examination of the changing structure of the organization is possible through the use of inventory data. The changing skill and quality mix can be determined from historical information. The current inventory, therefore, should be designed to facilitate possible future analytical studies.

A fourth criterion involves making the inventory exercise a relatively simple and inexpensive task. It is possible to design an inventory that requires operating management to furnish information that involves a considerable amount of money and effort. A job analysis and position requirement exercise fits this category and, if undertaken, would be useful in clarifying organizational relationships and in compensation. Too much inventory information may overwhelm the analyst and never receive attention. Or, the inventory data may divert time that should be given to forecasting and planning. Finally, too much attention to inventory exercises may cause the organization to regard the manpower planning program as a "make work" exercise that is not economically sound.

PERSONNEL RESEARCH

One of the major implications of manpower planning is increased attention to personnel research. Establishment of objectives to guide the planning and programming work has been discussed. Lack of research information limits the ability to identify these objectives or to design programs that will be effective in meeting current or potential problems.

Large organizations are able to utilize full-time personnel researchers to help in the management of manpower. Smaller organizations frequently believe that they are unable to employ full-time researchers because of financial constraints. Whatever the size of the organization, a research attitude to manpower problems is needed. Many such problems cannot be solved through reliance on existing information or knowledge. A willingness to spend time and money on serious investigation of the firm's individual problems and conditions can yield excellent returns on the investments.

The typical full-time personnel researcher is trained in research methodology, has an interest in depth analysis of situations, and is free from daily administrative decision-making responsibilities. His training is probably in industrial or organizational psychology or sociology because of the behavioral aspects of manpower management. This narrow mix of academic training in personnel research, it is hoped, will change in the future. An inter-disciplinary approach, such as that involved in the operations reseach concept, offers great potential for personnel research. Economists, engineers, political scientists, mathematicians, and business administrators can provide useful insights and knowledge on manpower research problems.[9] One of the major advantages of introducing a variety of disciplines into the reseach effort is to help to assure that the problems and situations under study are correctly identified and defined. Like any other specialist, the behavioral scientist has certain "trained incapacities" which limit his ability to perceive and interpret events.

The current manpower research efforts in business, educational, military, and other organizations range from efforts to construct simulation models of the manpower structure of organizations to studies of how various types of values held by

[9] The United States Air Force, for example, has used applied mathematicians to develop models that help analyze the career flows of air force personnel over long time periods. The solution to a question of whether to accelerate the promotion rate of airmen to meet 1969 manpower needs was determined by one such model. Paper delivered by Colonel [Dr.] James H. Ritter, "Recent Personnel Research in the U.S. Air Force: A Review," delivered at the Twenty-Fifth Anniversary Symposium on Personnel Research and Systems Advancement (unclassified), sponsored by USAF 6570th Personnel Research Laboratory, Lackland Air Force Base, San Antonio, Texas, November 1-3, 1966.

managers may have impact on the operational meaning of professed management objectives.[10]

One area of manpower research is the nature of the dynamics of the management manpower structure. How does it change over time? What causes it to change? How should it change for optimum results? A related problem area is that of ways to anticipate future organizational design requirements. What are the factors (aside from personalities) which are especially influential in shaping particular designs? What data can be used to predict how organizational units will grow or contract in the future? How is computer and information technology affecting the design of the organization?

A third area to which added attention should be given is that of ways in which the external environment influences an organization's manpower system. Our attention is usually directed to economic consequences of environmental changes in technology, government regulation, and competition, but how do changing social norms influence managerial attitudes and norms? What are the implications of the student unrest on college campuses for the business firm in the future? Have organization manpower managers given enough attention to the implications of the increasing desires and opportunities of persons for leisure? Do manpower managers really understand the implications of the problems, forces, and trends in the area of race relations that are affecting the organization? If the persons responsible for manpower management do not concern themselves with questions of this nature, who in the organization does possess an understanding of the changing environment?

This chapter has given a number of examples of directed personnel research efforts. These examples are not used solely to illustrate the richness or sophistication of the methodology the professionally trained researcher brings to his tasks. The majority are examples of how a research attitude plus modest investigation and effort can result in more intelligent decision-making, in an increase in the quantity and quality research, and can generate greater professionalism in manpower management.

---

10 Dr. George England of the Industrial Relations Center of the University of Minnesota is engaged currently in studying the values held by managers.

CONCLUSION

Manpower planning action programs which are related to defined objectives help the organization meet manpower challenges with greater effectiveness. These challenges are revealed through analysis of the current and probable future manpower conditions in the organization. Some programs may have a very long-term payoff, while others will be of a more immediate nature. It is important in manpower planning efforts to have a mixture of the two types — a portfolio of programs with varying payoff periods. The short-run programs are important in gaining and maintaining acceptance and support for manpower planning; the long-run programs help the organization overcome basic structural problems that cannot be corrected immediately.

The emphasis in the discussion in this chapter has been on describing the nature of programs in individual areas of manpower planning. These programs have strong interrelationships, however, and should also be interpreted in light of their potential impact on each other. Thus, a "general systems" type of mentality is required to design and implement manpower action programs. Although the major thrust of a given program will be at a particular need or problem, the program designer must be aware of the simultaneous impact of the program on other activities, and of the potential "follow-on" consequences of the program once it has been initiated.

Because manpower planning programs are frequently designed to help relieve potential problems, they will not always be successful. When the problem is still somewhat distant in time, it may not be so clearly recognizable or defined as when it is an immediate concern. This situation may result in some decision errors in plans for coping with the potential problem or need, especially when experimental approaches are adopted. It is important to remember that whenever one plans to meet the future and tries to innovate he may experience failure, but that the net result of the planning and innovation should contribute to much greater success in the final analysis of performance.

CHAPTER 3 APPENDIX

CAREER MOBILITY PROGRAMS

The design of career mobility programs is neither a refined practice nor is it something that once accomplished is immune from further revisions. As organizational objectives and activities change from time to time, the type of managers needed to occupy important positions changes. Some of the factors the manpower planner might consider in designing career mobility programs are discussed below.

1. The career mobility program should provide opportunities for managers to acquire the organizational knowledge and managerial skills that will be important to them in the future.

Information relevant to these criteria is gained by determining the knowledge and skills especially important to current top managers and key middle managers. The planner attempts to ascertain the direction of managerial practices and techniques (e.g., increased use of mathematical decision-making models) to gain a feeling for future requirements.

The knowledge factor pertains to understanding what the manager does in such activities as marketing administration, budget planning and control, systems analysis, and general manufacturing. The skills factor relates to the importance of various skills (e.g., motivating others, decision-making under uncertainty, policy formulation) in performing managerial tasks.

2. The program should attempt to make the best use of the learning and development opportunities in the organization.

Here the concern is with where in the organization a manager can best acquire the knowledge and skills considered important. Do lower level managers in finance really acquire knowledge and experience that is useful later in their careers? Is decision-making best learned in line organizational elements, or is this a myth fostered by tradition? Which activities best provide breadth of knowledge, and which provide desired specialized knowledge? If it is important for a manager to know how to motivate others effectively, where in the organization can this skill be best acquired? How important are managers in helping subordinates acquire knowledge and skill? Are some of the managers particularly good at developing men, and if so are they used effectively in this regard?

3. The program should insure that a manager acquires sufficient depth of knowledge in an activity to perform effectively at higher levels of responsibility in that activity.

The manpower planner must determine the amount of knowledge of an activity a manager should have to occupy positions at different levels in an organizational unit. For example, can a person perform at middle management in finance without any prior experience in finance? If this is not possible, how much experience does he need for effective performance? If it is possible to perform well without previous experience, is this in terms of a few selective positions or in a rather broad set of positions? What are the comparable situations in production, marketing, and general administration?

4. The program should insure that the organization is capable of using a man in an effective manner throughout his career.

Most organizations will eventually utilize many managers in particular fields of specialization because of the need to have middle management experts in these fields. Because of this, it is important that the career mobility program provide a manager with a specialization that can be used by the organization in placing him in the latter portion of his career. The program should produce more than generalists who lack ability to manage and administer effectively in a specialized field.

5. The program should attempt to insure that the acquisition of knowledge (general and in depth) and skills is sequenced over time in an effective manner.

This criterion once again focuses on the learning process and how to make it efficient. If a manager can perform at middle management in finance without prior finance experience, what combination of previous experiences is most useful for him to have had? Is it especially helpful for a man to have had good training in analytical work (perhaps gained in a staff job) before he is given major decision-making responsibilities?

Does experience in making decisions prior to staff analytical training increase the appreciation for thorough analysis, or does it create an impression that analysis is not important because of past successes in making minor decisions without taking time for analysis?

6. Initial placement of young college hires should be compatible with the career mobility program.

The initial job may be the first step in a general career program. It may be a testing area to determine if the organization should retain the new hire for long-run utilization. Or, again, it may be an evaluation position to determine whether the new hire receives attention in a career mobility program. Whatever the objective of initial placement, it should relate to longer-run manpower utilization factors. This means chance vacancies should not be relied upon for placing new hires in the organization; entry point vacancies can be engineered through promotions and transfers. The objective is to insure that a certain number of desired openings are available each year for new hires.

7. The organization design and management staffing structure should provide support for the mobility pattern program.

The planner cannot engineer the design of the organization solely around the need to provide good career progressions for managers, but he can be aware of career mobility factors in the design of the organization. The addition of another management layer in the organization may be either desirable or undesirable from a career management point of view. It may provide a good testing area for future top managers, or it may provide valuable experience for these persons. On the other hand, it may not be useful as a development position and would instead result in an extension of organization and communication lines that dilute the significance of the lower positions. Similarly, a relatively flat organization may provide good training and development opportunities, a fact which may cause resistance to the addition of new organization layers that would otherwise be desirable from a control standpoint.

This discussion has focused on the developmental aspects of career mobility programs for individuals. It is not suggested that attempts be made to plan careers for individual managers for a given number of years into the future. Rather, what is implied is that when vacancies arise, the long-run benefits of assigning a particular individual to the position will be considered. Likewise, the planner should regularly examine what is happening to individual managers in their careers to determine if they are receiving the organizational training and development that will make them valuable managers in the long run.

A mobility pattern program also considers the speed at which a manager can progress upward without hurting the organization or damaging his own long-term usefulness. It provides men with exposure to a variety of superiors in different activities and thus gives opportunities to learn good managerial techniques from each superior as well as what management practices to avoid.

Mobility pattern programs should also permit the organization to gain evaluation information on its managers from a variety of sources. Are managers rated above average in one activity as capable as those who are similarly rated in another activity? Does the firm have managers who can perform well in several functions? Does it need to develop specialists in an activity in order to obtain good performance there?

Such programs also permit individuals to display talents that might otherwise be hidden if the men are confirmed to a narrow set of activities throughout their careers. It is possible for an above-average finance manager to have talents hidden or not utilized in that activity. These talents might perhaps enable him to be a superior manager in the marketing function.

A final benefit of a mobility program is the added depth it provides to the management structure. Having men capable of filling vacancies in other departments because of prior broadening experience may reduce the necessity of recruiting from the outside or of filling a position with the only candidate available internally. Thus it may be possible to avoid the situation of having only one qualified candidate for a position because of minimum experience requirements associated with the vacancy. To have five or six men worthy of serious consideration is better assurance that the best talent does in fact move upward in the organization.

CHAPTER 4

ANALYZING MANAGERIAL MANPOWER
REQUIREMENTS

...forecasting, planning, and control are not simple, clear-cut operations to be carried out by one or a few persons within a single department.... They may be likened to a symphony — a symphony performed not by musicians but by operating personnel, industrial engineers, production-planning engineers, quality-control engineers, and purchasing and accounting executives.

— E. H. MacNiece

One manpower planner describes his overall goal as that of insuring a constant supply of highly qualified persons for top management jobs. He focuses attention on the intake of new persons, their upward flow rate in management, and the points at which they leave the organization.

This type of examination provides insights into the dynamics of the organization and its structure. It helps the planner to understand how the current stock of manpower relates to the stock forcast for the future. He is concerned with the proper management of the manpower flow between these stock points to enable his organization to have talent available when and where it is needed.

The concern is not confined solely to top management manpower needs. The manpower planner mentioned above is located at the corporate headquarters of one of the world's largest corporations. His attention is devoted to corporate-wide top management needs. At each operating division in the company, attention is given to middle and lower level management staffing.

To give assistance in understanding the dynamics of managerial staffing is the objective of this chapter. A methodologi-

95

cal approach is illustrated through the description of a hypothetical company (Company Y) and its manpower structure.

The statistics used in the example have been constructed to assist in the illustration of the method presented. They also are designed to direct attention to certain kinds of manpower problems. Although these numbers are hypothetical, they are not unrealistic. Some of the age, educational, and organizational relationships portrayed have been observed in American companies.[1]

With respect to the diagram of the manpower planning process shown in Chapter 2, the material in this chapter relates to Step 1-A, "Management Inventory" and Step 5, "Management Manpower Estimates." The analysis as outlined leads to some of the considerations involved in the setting of manpower objectives and in the design of action programs discussed in Chapter 3.

THE NATURE OF COMPANY Y

Because this book is intended for use by planners in operating units or departments of a company as well as by the overall manpower planner, Company Y is presented as a wholly owned subsidiary of a large corporation. Transfer of manpower between units in the organization thus can be included in the discussion, for these transfers frequently affect manpower planning work at the subsidiary, division, and department levels.

The assumption is that Company Y has a line and staff organization and engages in manpower forecasting and planning. Its recent manpower efforts have been aimed at developing a stock of young college-educated managers to help meet impending middle management retirements that will be more numerous than normal. These efforts have meant the hiring of upwards of 70 college men in a year and advancing them rather rapidly. The management analysis takes place in the summer after new hires have been placed in the organization, but prior to the next college recruiting season. Because of the retirement situation in Company Y during the next decade, a ten-year manpower forecast and analysis is desired.

---

[1] Scientists and engineers are included in the manpower figures used in the illustration. Companies with large numbers of engineers might study them independently of the overall manpower classification.

The example is directed primarily at the examination of four factors:

1. The nature of the manpower flow in the organization.
2. The problems associated with determining the number of college graduates who should be used for staffing lower management positions.
3. The development of college recruiting quotas.
4. The identification of management development and promotion problems in the company.

The analysis focuses on male management personnel. It is assumed that females occupy salaried-exempt positions in Company Y but in order to simplify the exposition they are not discussed separately. Attrition rates and progression patterns of females may differ substantially from those of males, and may prompt separate studies of female employment patterns by companies which have many female managers. Such analyses may become more important at Title VII (the "equal opportunity" section) of the Civil Rights Act of 1964 is interpreted and applied.

THE MANPOWER INVENTORY

An annual inventory of current manpower is the starting point in the analysis of managerial manpower. This inventory reveals the nature of the manpower structure by age, education, performance quality, promotion potential, and organization unit and level. It also indicates the manpower that will be available throughout the planning period and at the end of the period.

The initial arrangement of the data as shown in Table 4-1 is organized by five-year age intervals, organization level, and educational attainment. The five-year age interval is useful in planning, but another interval might be desirable if the planning period is for less than five years. Organizational levels are determined by the payroll structure or some other kind of managerial classification. In Company Y, Levels 1 to 3 are considered lower management, Levels 4 to 6 middle management, and Levels 7 to 9 top management. The educational attainment criterion is whether or not a manager has a college degree. The increased utilization of college graduates throughout management argues for the adoption of this type of

TABLE 4-1

MANAGEMENT INVENTORY – COMPANY Y

Level	Age Interval									Total All Ages
	20-24	25-29	30-34	35-39	40-44	45-49	50-54	55-59	60-64	
9	—	—	—	—	—	—	—	1	—	1
8	—	—	—	—	—	2	1	1 (1)	1 (1)	5 (2)
7	—	—	—	—	5	7 (1)	7 (2)	9 (3)	6 (2)	34 (8)
6	—	—	—	5	10	15 (5)	15 (10)	30 (15)	20 (10)	95 (40)
5	—	—	—	10	20 (5)	20 (10)	20 (10)	25 (30)	30 (20)	125 (75)
4	—	—	10	25 (5)	30 (10)	20 (20)	15 (30)	35 (30)	30 (20)	165 (115)
3	—	15	30	55 (10)	40 (25)	25 (20)	30 (30)	10 (25)	5 (25)	210 (135)
2	5	40	45 (10)	(30)	(70)	(70)	(60)	(60)	(70)	90 (370)
1	10	20	15 (15)	(75)	(55)	(80)	(50)	(75)	(65)	45 (415)
College Trainees (TR)	35	35								70
Total: All Levels	50	110	100 (25)	95 (120)	105 (165)	89 (206)	88 (192)	111 (239)	92 (213)	840 (1160)
Total: TR to 3	50	110	90 (25)	55 (115)	40 (150)	25 (170)	30 (140)	10 (160)	5 (160)	415 (920)
Total: 4 to 9	—	—	10 —	40 (5)	65 (15)	64 (36)	58 (52)	101 (79)	87 (53)	425 (240)

NOTE: Figures in parentheses indicate men without a college education, figures without parentheses are men with college degrees.

classification although other firms may need a different type of classification.

In Company Y a heavy concentration of managers exists in the 55- to 64-year age interval. In lower management, the upcoming retirees are all men without degrees — indication of a need for many new first and second level supervisors from the hourly ranks unless staffing patterns are changed. The distribution of manpower by education shows the different career patterns of the two categories. College graduates begin in management at lower ages and move up in the organization rather rapidly. This may be the result of a lack of attention to capable younger hourly employees until they have been employed for ten or more years and have made themselves gradually visible over time.

The inventory is not concerned with individual managers — the emphasis is on total manpower resources. Examination of individual career situations is reserved to the action programming work discussed in Chapter 3. The task in the managerial manpower analysis is to identify problems and establish objectives for the entire management structure.

PROJECTING MANPOWER LOSSES

The overall expected loss situation is examined in Table 4-2. Here ten-year estimates of retirements, net transfer losses, and losses due to other causes are totaled to determine the number of current personnel who will still be employed in ten years. The figures indicate that of the 2,000 current managers, only 1,090 are expected to be available after ten years. Fifty per cent of the top managers and 48 per cent of the middle managers will have retired by that time. (This is perhaps an above-average middle management retirement loss, but it is less than that experienced by some American companies in a ten-year period.)

Early retirements are included in the "Other Losses" category. They are based on actuarial data on losses for various age groups furnished by pension and life insurance underwriters. The table would cover losses due to early retirements, deaths, disability, and other factors. A table which covers losses for five-year age intervals by organization level is very helpful.

TABLE 4-2

ESTIMATES OF TEN-YEAR MANAGEMENT LOSSES – COMPANY Y

Level	Current Manpower		Retirements (Regular)		Transfer Losses (Net)	Other Losses		Total Losses		Expected Available Manpower	
9	1	—	1	—	—	—	—	1	—	—	—
8	5	(2)	2	(2)	—	—	—	2	(2)	3	—
7	34	(8)	15	(5)	—	2	—	17	(5)	17	(3)
6	95	(40)	50	(25)	1	9	(3)	60	(28)	35	(12)
5	125	(75)	55	(50)	2	18	(5)	75	(55)	50	(20)
4	165	(115)	65	(50)	4	16	(15)	85	(65)	80	(50)
3	210	(135)	15	(40)	10	30	(20)	55	(60)	155	(75)
2	90	(370)	—	(130)	—	15	(40)	15	(170)	75	(200)
1	45	(415)	—	(140)	—	15	(45)	15	(185)	30	(230)
TR	70	—	—	—	—	15	—	15	—	55	—
Total	840	(1,160)	203	(442)	17	120	(128)	340	(570)	500	(590)

Other Losses include quits, terminations, deaths, disabilities, and early retirements.

If the manpower planner lacks such a table he will have to develop his own expected loss rates. This is done by examining past experience and modifying the information in light of changes in hiring standards, medical benefit programs, and such factors that influence early retirements as changes in pension plans or government social and health insurance plans.

Transfer losses are shown on a net basis. They are based on past experience and estimates of future manpower demands on the organization by the parent company. Information on the gross additions and losses as well as the net figure is important in this examination. Although Company Y is expecting to have a net transfer loss of ten Level 3 managers, it might actually lose 15 highly qualified persons and receive five average performers through "transfers in."

The transfer losses are examined by organizational level, promotion potential, and the organization unit involved. One department, such as engineering, might be a regular exporter of talent, while finance or personnel might be a regular importer of talent. The amount of analysis given transfers is governed by their volume and their impact on the organization. Information from the study of transfers is useful in designing manpower programs that will help build equilibrum into the manpower structure and in determining organization entry points for new manpower.

STAFFING THE FUTURE ORGANIZATION

Examination of the nature of the future organization begins with the breakdown of the manpower forecast into major wage categories (Table 4-3). Trend data and information on probable future changes are used to make the projections. Historical data may reveal strong trends resulting from factors that are expected to exist in the future. Automation, for example, has meant fewer hourly jobs relative to total employment in many companies. The numbers developed for Company Y reflect this factor, as seen by a slight contraction of the hourly group relative to total employment.

A similiar analysis is used to estimate the future composition of management. Trends in the management structure in the firm and in other companies are studied to aid in making

TABLE 4-3

OCCUPATIONAL STAFFING — COMPANY Y

Level	Present		Year Ten	
	Number	Per Cent	Number	Per Cent
Hourly	6,500	65	6,000	63
Non-Exempt Salaried	1,500	15	1,400	15
Managerial	2,000	20	2,100	22
Total	10,000	100	9,500	100

TABLE 4-4

ORGANIZATIONAL COMPOSITION OF MANAGEMENT — COMPANY Y

Management Level	Present		Year Ten	
	Number	Per Cent	Number	Per Cent
Top	50	2	60	3
Middle	615	31	670	32
Lower	1,335	67	1,370	65
Total	2,000	100	2,100	100

these estimates. Knowledge of the creation of new operations (e.g., an international division) and technological pressures for changes in the organization design (e.g., computer technological and information systems) can influence the judgments. In Company Y estimates are made for the top, middle, and lower management levels by percentage of the total management workforce in order to reach a total manpower estimate in these groups (Table 4-4). These groups are further divided by relative percentages to make a numerical estimate of manpower at each organization level (Table 4-5). The percentage figures to use in this type of estimation are difficult to determine. Information for the future from manpower coordinators in the operating units is helpful. Utilization of trend data modified by information on potential organization changes is perhaps the method most commonly used.

The Future of Middle Management

There is a great deal of speculation on the future nature, size, and growth of middle management. Much of the discussion centers on the long-run consequences of advances in information technology. The impact of the computer and its information-processing and analytical capabilities upon management is not fully known. Recentralization of operations made possible by computer systems has eliminated some middle management jobs. At the same time, because of the computer, new specialists are appearing at or near middle

TABLE 4-5

ORGANIZATIONAL COMPOSITION (BY LEVELS) OF
MANAGEMENT — COMPANY Y

Level	Present		Year Ten	
	Number	Per Cent	Number	Per Cent
9	1		1	
8	7	2	9	3
7	42		50	
6	135	7	145	7
5	200	10	230	11
4	280	14	295	14
3	345	18	380	18
2	460	23	465	22
1 and TR	530	26	525	25
Total	2,000	100	2,100	100

NOTE: Numbers and percentages are rounded to facilitate illustration.

management in sophisticated planning and control work. Often the activities are new ones or else were previously performed at a rather low level of sophistication. Operations researchers, economic analysts and forecasters, market researchers, and systems specialists, are examples of this type of talent.[2]

One of the major activities of these management specialists is to assist in the decision-making process by determining the significance of data, by identifying problems, and by monitoring the results of decisions. Their role is frequently that of furnishing information to higher management for decision-making, and to operating management on the results of activities. Management specialists, however, may have little if any role in the implementation of decisions. The upgraded quality of decisions that results from their efforts may reduce the number of managers, particularly middle managers, who are responsible for decision implementation. The specialists' reporting relationships to top management may be so close that they appear to occupy middle management positions, yet they may receive lower salaries than the middle managers in the line organization.

An important characteristic of these management specialists is that they come closer to being "professional" persons than do the traditional line or staff managers. Their sophisticated training and experience have given them a basic knowledge discipline. Their loyalties to their discipline may be as strong, or stronger, than to the organization. They have a tendency, therefore, to leave an organization if they believe they will enhance their professional development elsewhere or if they believe their efforts are not adequately appreciated. Because

---

[2] For some contrasting views on this subject see: J. F. Burlingam, "Information Technology and Decentralization," *Harvard Business Review* (November-December 1961); Harold J. Leavitt and Thomas L. Whisler, "Management Will Never be the Same Again," *Fortune* (August 1964); "The Other Side of Automation," *Dun's Review* (May 1962); and P. B. Schoderbek, and C. G. Schoderbek, "The New Manager?" *Systems and Procedures Journal* (July-August 1965). A rather thorough examination of the impact of information technology on the firm is contained in *Management Organization and the Computer* by George P. Schultz and Thomas L. Whisler (Chicago: Free Press of Glencoe, 1960). Experiences of five companies with computer information systems are presented by company spokesmen and discussed by other members of a seminar gathered to discuss the problems posed by the title of the book.

of their transferable knowledge, they are able to move more freely to other organizations than the works manager, the sales manager, or the general administration supervisor. The problems associated with the management of scientists and engineers will, therefore, be encountered with increasing frequency among these management specialists.

When engineering and scientific positions are included in the definition of the management group (as in this book) the author is led to believe that middle management type positions will increase relative to lower management jobs. This is because of the predicted growth in professional jobs and the tendency for a narrower organizational span of control in the professional hierarchy.

Among the firms surveyed for information on manpower planning, lower management jobs appeared more vulnerable to displacement by technological advances than middle management positions. This was especially true when automation reduced the number of hourly or clerical personnel to be supervised. In addition, professional jobs were growing at levels comparable in salary and status to middle management and several marketing organizations were upgrading their sales activities to a more professional status. Many of the new type of salesmen occupied a position above that of a first level production manager.

The projected future management structure of Company Y reflects a leaning towards relatively more middle managers (or their counterparts in engineering). As additional evidence on middle management's future becomes available this view might change. Planners should examine available information regarding middle management's future role in their companies carefully when estimating future manpower needs at this level.

Projected Educational Background of Managers

The estimate of the probable educational backgrounds of future managers at various levels is used to help determine college recruiting needs and to administer the upward flow of talent in the organization. In most companies, more college graduates are now being used to fill management positions than in the past.[3] Previous trend data and information on the current promotability of managers according to educational background are combined in making estimates. The current educational staffing pattern and the projected middle and top management pattern for Company Y are shown in Table 4-6. Because lower management positions filled by college graduates are dependent on college recruiting quotas, the determination of the composition of this management level cannot be made until college recruiting requirements are established. For this reason, Levels 1 to 3 are not projected in Table 4-6.

DETERMINING COLLEGE RECRUITING REQUIREMENTS

The method used by many companies to determine college recruiting quotas is relatively simple, as outlined below. A more complicated alternative to this method is then presented. The second approach is preferred by the author because it adopts as a basic premise the belief that current college recruiting influences the manpower structure for 30 or 40 years into the future. It also rests on the premise that the availability of manpower for future top and middle management positions is influenced by current college recruiting. These two premises force the manpower planner into establishing recruiting quotas on the basis of very long-run considerations.

The Expected-vacancy Method

The determination of college recruiting needs during the manpower planning period by this method is linked to an estimate of future manpower needs and to a comparison of these needs with the expected available manpower based on current resources. The differences in the two estimates determine intake requirements.

---

[3] In one company, the number of non-college men reaching a middle management position dropped significantly in a short time period. Of the men currently employed who reached this position prior to 1960, over 55 per cent lacked a degree. Since 1960, only 22 per cent of the men reaching the position lacked a degree. In addition, only one of the 29 men rated promotable to the position in 1965 lacked a degree, and this man had only a slim chance of being promoted because age considerations were working against him.

TABLE 4-6

MANAGERIAL STAFFING BY LEVEL AND EDUCATION – COMPANY Y

Level	Present				Year Ten			
	College		Non-college		College		Non-college	
	Per Cent	Number	Per Cent	Number	Per Cent	Number	Per Cent	Number
9	100	1	—	—	100	1	—	—
8	70	5	30	2	90	8	10	1
7	80	34	20	8	90	45	10	5
6	70	95	30	40	80	115	20	30
5	60	125	40	75	70	160	30	70
4	60	165	40	115	70	205	30	90
3	61	210	39	135	—	—	—	—
2	20	90	80	370	—	—	—	—
1 and TR	22	115	78	415	—	—	—	—
Total	47	840	53	1,160	73	534	27	196

In Company Y this analysis centers on middle and top management because lower management jobs for college graduates are pipeline positions into higher responsibilities. Company Y forecasts a need for 534 college graduates at middle and top management at the end of ten years (from Table 4-6). The company expects to have 500 college graduates available in ten years (from Table 4-2). Thus from these estimates it needs to hire 34 men in the next ten years for middle and top management positions. In addition, it has 415 college men currently in lower management who presumably will need replacement to raise the total to 449 new college men to recruit. Provision for early separation and failure to obtain middle management positions due to a variety of factors adds another nine men to the total intake requirement. (The determination of provisions for these factors is discussed below.) A total of 458 men are thus needed from the college recruiting program as calculated by the expected-vacancy method.

The Career-utilization Method

This approach to the problem of quota determination for college recruiting is an attempt to produce greater stability in the eventual retirement pattern of managers and to avoid serious potential recruiting errors. The results obtained with the Company Y data do not differ significantly from those of the expected-vacancy method. The assumptions used, however, are more clearly related to future needs. The planner does not, for example, assume he should recruit men for lower level management just to duplicate the current staffing pattern. If he follows that logic he may seriously under- or over-recruit because the current staffing at lower management may or may not be suitable for the future higher level requirements.

Two steps are involved in determining recruiting needs by this method. The first is the recognition that new hiring is influenced by far distant staffing requirements of middle and top management. In examining prospects for the far distant future (e.g., 30 years ahead), company Y concludes that college graduates will occupy nearly all the middle and top management jobs — a higher percentage than is forecast for ten years ahead. The current college recruiting program therefore should be related to these very distant needs.

In Company Y it is estimated that by the time new college hires are in top management, all the vacancies at this level will be filled by college graduates. This compares with the ten-year outlook of 90 per cent staffing by college men. In middle management, the long-term outlook is for 90 per cent staffing by college men versus the 73 per cent now estimated at the end of ten years.

The second step in this process involves a determination of the number of very long-term positions to hire against during the current manpower planning period. New manpower should be hired to fill top management positions, but for how many of these positions should they be recruited? To determine this it is necessary to know the age at which the average top manager reaches that level and how long he serves in top management. The same information is needed for the managers who plateau-out at middle management.

In Company Y a manpower objective is to have the average top manager who has a college degree reach that level by approximately age 47 and to occupy a top position for about 15 years. This means, then, that in every ten-year period, two-thirds of the top management group will retire. In middle management, the Company Y objective is to have a man reach lower middle management by approximately age 33 and to have an average tenure of about 25 years. Thus, in the average ten-year period, 40 per cent of the middle managers will retire.

These career progression rates for Company Y indicate that for the positions to be filled by college graduates, 66 per cent of the future top managers and 40 per cent of the future middle managers should be recruited during a ten-year college recruiting period.

At this point, however, there is no estimate of the total number of middle and top management positions that will exist in the very long run. The manpower forecasting technique outlined in Chapters 5 and 6 relies on output estimates of the organization. Since it is unlikely that the organization makes such estimates beyond ten years, the ability to forecast these very long-run positions is greatly reduced.

To generate the data needed for such a manpower forecast is almost certain to be an uneconomic venture, for the cost of the data will outweigh their economic usefulness. Even speculation on the manpower structure 30 years into the future, independent of any forecasting model, also appears uneconomic. This is especially true when few, if any, persons in the organization are qualified to engage in this type of speculation. Looking 30 years into the future means attempting to cope with a tremendous number of unknowns. At this stage of knowledge of organizational growth the planner would appear to be better off without the information. The exception to this statement is, of course, when the need to have the data is so crucial to the company's survival that data must be generated regardless of cost. The type of company manpower information discussed here does not fit this criterion.

The planner is forced, nevertheless, into recognizing that current recruiting efforts should anticipate very long-range manpower utilization patterns. The top managers of tomorrow are among the new hires. He also must recognize that to accomplish his objective of determining college recruiting needs he will not be able to use some data he would like to have because they are not available.

To resolve this dilemma he may fall back on what is called a "satisficing" approach to the problem. This approach recognizes that he is unable to achieve all that he desires in the situation and that a satisfactory type of solution is required. His solution is considered to be generally adequate, considering the amount of information available.

He uses, therefore, the manpower forecast made for the future (the ten-year forecast in the Company Y case) as his best estimate of still longer range needs, while recognizing that there may be either additional or fewer managerial positions in the time periods beyond the forecast horizon. If he is quite certain of more distant trends, he might wish to modify the forecast upward or downward. Without this information, however, the forecast serves as the basic figure. Because this forecast is revised each year, the necessary adjustments to the very long-range staffing needs can be made gradually.

Returning to the specifics of the Company Y situation, the following information is now available.

a. The ten-year manpower forecast indicates a need for 60 top managers. This serves as a reference point for very long-range needs against which estimates will be made. Eventually all these positions will be filled with college graduates. Two-thirds of future top managers should be recruited in a ten-year period: that is, 40 men in the next ten years for eventual utilization at top management (60 positions x 100 per cent college staffing x 67 per cent ten-year turnover).

b. In middle management the base figure is for 670 middle management positions in the long run, with college graduates eventually to staff 90 per cent of the positions. To replace 40 per cent of the middle managers every ten years Company Y, therefore, will need to recruit 240 men for eventual middle management careers during the next ten years (670 positions x 90 per cent college staffing x 40 per cent ten-year turnover).

The complications of this procedure are avoided, as mentioned above, by organizations that merely recruit against expected vacancies in the planning period. For a growing organization with a changing mix of college to non-college educated managers, the expected-vacancy method may quickly create a manpower shortage. Its adoption rests upon its simplicity instead of upon the recognition of the long-run needs of the organization.

Early Losses of College Hires

Another factor in estimating college recruiting requirements is need to provide for early losses of new hires for voluntary or induced reasons. Another objective of Company Y for the period is to hold this loss rate during the first ten years of employment to an average of 30 per cent of those hired in a year. The company expects that two-thirds of the separations will occur in the first five years of employment and the other one-third in the second five years. After the initial ten years of employment, losses are expected to conform to actuarial experiences. Holding the early attrition rate to 30 per cent is a major objective because of the costs associated with recruitment and early development of college manpower.

Provision for a 30 per cent loss rate for the 280 men eventually needed for middle and top management means that an additional 120 men will have to be recruited during the ten-year period to cover these anticipated losses (280/1.0 - .30).

In addition to these losses, the company expects that it will inevitably hire men who will not reach middle management even though they are carefully evaluated during their early employment. In Company Y, the objective is to hold this loss at ten per cent of the new hires who will remain with the company. This means that approximately 30 men should be recruited during the next ten years to provide for this type of fallout (280/1.0 - .10).

Total College Recruitment Needs

The analysis developed for Company Y indicates a college recruiting need of 430 men during the next ten years, broken down as follows:

— 40 men for eventual use at top management.
— 240 men for eventual use at middle management.
— 120 men as provision for early attrition.
— 30 men as a provision for below-average progress.

The Recruiting Quota Pattern

To help establish the pattern of recruiting, a comparison is made of the total vacancies expected in ten years with the estimated intake requirement developed by the "career-utilization" approach. In Company Y, 534 middle and top management positions are projected to be filled by college graduates in year ten (Table 4-6). Estimates of future losses indicate that 500 of the current managers will be available to fill these positions. Of these men 30, however, are not regarded as having middle management potential, which means that only 470 current managers will be available. Thus an estimated shortage of 65 men (actually 64 rounded to 65 to simplify exposition) for middle management will exist in year ten as based on current manpower. This deficiency does not alter the total recruiting needs of Company Y; the intake schedule of 280 men is designed to insure that 65 of the men will be ready for middle management in year ten.

Examination of the career development paths of new hires is made to determine how the recruiting intake schedule should be designed to provide these 65 men. Company Y's early development program for new managers calls for the new hire to spend his first year in a trainee classification. This is a trial or early evaluation position equivalent to a first level manager. If the man is considered worthy of continued employment, he will spend another year in first line management and then be promoted to second level. Three years are planned as the normal length of time at both Levels 2 and 3. Therefore if new college hires are recruited on a uniform basis during each year of the ten-year period, about 20 per cent will be in Trainee and Level 1 positions; 30 per cent at Level 2; and 30 per cent at Level 3. The other 20 per cent will have reached middle management Level 4. Because these are average progression rates, individual men will spend shorter or longer periods in each position depending on their performance and the need to fill vacancies.

The progression and expected loss rates in lower management indicate that of the 430 new hires, approximately 56 men will have progressed to middle management Level 4 if men are recruited on a uniform basis (i.e., 43 men each year for ten years). It has been seen, however, that 65 of the men hired during the period should reach middle management by year ten. To overcome this potential shortage of nine men, Company Y must recruit an above-average number of men in the first few years of the period.

The theoretical quotas developed for Company Y (shown in Table 4-7) include consideration of the career progression rate, the early attrition expected, and the below-average performance of some of the men hired. The quotas provide for above-average recruiting in the first few years with balanced recruiting after that period.

Lower Management Staffing

The expected distribution of this manpower by management level is also determined by the average progression rate, early attrition, and provision for below-average performance. Table 4-8 shows how the manpower from the recruiting quota is expected to be distributed in year ten.

TABLE 4-7

COLLEGE RECRUITING QUOTA DETERMINATION —
COMPANY Y

Year Recruited	Men Recruited for Middle and Upper Management	Men Recruited for Probable Platooning at Lower Management	Men Recruited to Provide for Early Attrition	Total Manpower Recruited
1	35	4	15	54
2	30	3	13	46
3	30	3	13	46
4	25	3	11	39
5	25	3	11	39
6	30	3	12	45
7	25	3	11	39
8	25	2	11	38
9	30	3	12	45
10	25	3	11	39
Total	280	30	120	430

The lower management positions occupied by college hires are "channel" positions to middle management. All lower management positions in Company Y not required for channel use are to be filled by non-college men (Table 4-9). Included in the table are the 30 managers already in the workforce who are not expected to reach middle management. A summary of the projected management staffing for all levels by educational background is shown in Table 4-10. The comparison of expected needs by education and current available resources is shown in Table 4-11. The new manpower needs reflect projected deficiencies (or surpluses as shown by parentheses). Available manpower is shown by the current position rather than position anticipated at the end of the ten years.

QUALITATIVE MANPOWER CONSIDERATIONS

A qualitative view of the existing managerial manpower is gained through a Promotion Potential Table (Table 4-12). All men with potential for advancement of one or two levels during the next ten years are shown by their current ages and levels. (Tables such as these set up on a departmental basis may indicate an oversupply of talent in some units and at the same time shortages in other units).

The focus in the analysis of promotion potential is on men who will be with the organization at the end of the forecast period. Thus men 55 and over are excluded from the analysis because they will not be available as resources after year ten; however, these men are not considered as excluded from further promotions during the planning period.

Two promotion paths are drawn through Table 4-12. The upper line, the average progression path followed by men reaching top management, is developed from data on the progression of current top managers. The lower, or middle management promotion path, is developed in the same manner. These lines shift to the left or right as promotion rates accelerate or decrease. When first plotted they furnish information on mobility patterns in the organization, the impact of past management development programs, and the loss of top quality men to other organizations. Because individual departments usually have promotion patterns which differ from the overall pattern, they should be studied to determine their advantages and disadvantages, and their impact on the overall managerial structure. The promotion paths can also be considered with salary maturity curves used in salary administration for comparability and trend.

The numbers entered to the left of the upper promotion path indicate men progressing at a rate suitable for attainment of top management positions. Numbers to the right of the lower path indicate men who are considered promotable, but are progressing at a rate slower than the average. A comparison of the numbers in these areas with the total managerial group shown in Table 4-1 provides information for management development. The differences reflect the number of men by age and level who are not promotable. This may indicate a need for special development work for a certain age group or a certain level. (Separate tables may be required for engi-

TABLE 4-8

LOWER MANAGEMENT STAFFING DETERMINATION –
COMPANY Y

Year Recruited	Total Manpower Recruited	Expected Available Manpower in Year Ten	Expected Organizational Position of Manpower During Year Ten				
			Level				
			4	3	2	1	TR
1	54	39	35	1	3	–	–
2	46	34	25	7	2	–	–
3	46	33	5	20	8	–	–
4	39	29	–	21	8	–	–
5	39	29	–	18	11	–	–
6	45	35	–	13	22	–	–
7	39	30	–	–	30	–	–
8	38	31	–	–	31	–	–
9	45	40	–	–	–	40	–
10	39	35	–	–	–	–	35
Total	430	335	65	80	115	40	35
Current manpower platooned at level 3 (30)			–	30	–	–	–
Total manpower (365)			65	110	115	40	35

TABLE 4-9

YEAR TEN LOWER MANAGEMENT STAFFING – COMPANY Y

Level	College		Non-college		Total
	Per Cent	Number	Per Cent	Number	Number
3	29	110	71	270	380
2	25	115	75	350	465
1 and TR	14	75	86	450	525
Total	22	300	78	1,070	1,370

TABLE 4-10

EXPECTED TEN YEAR MANAGEMENT STAFFING BY
EDUCATION — COMPANY Y

Level	Expected Positions	College		Non-college	
	Number	Per Cent	Number	Per Cent	Number
9	1	90	1	10	—
8	9	90	8	10	1
7	50	90	45	10	5
6	145	80	115	20	30
5	230	80	160	20	70
4	295	70	205	30	90
3	380	29	110	71	270
2	465	25	115	75	350
1 and TR	525	14	75	86	450
Total	2,100	40	834	60	1,266

TABLE 4-11

EXPECTED NEW MANAGERS NEEDED TO FILL VACANCIES —
COMPANY Y

Level	Forecast Positions		Expected Manpower Available		New Manpower Needed	
	College	Non-college	College	Non-college	College	Non-college
9	1	—	—	—	1	—
8	8	1	3	—	5	1
7	45	5	17	3	28	2
6	115	30	35	12	80	18
5	160	70	50	20	110	50
4	205	90	80	50	125	40
3	110	270	155	75	(45)	195
2	115	350	75	200	40	150
1	40	450	30	230	10	220
TR	35	—	55	—	(20)	—
Total	834	1,266	500	590	334	676

TABLE 4-12

CURRENT PROMOTION POTENTIAL BY AGE AND LEVEL – COMPANY Y

Level	20-24 1*	20-24 2*	25-29 1	25-29 2	30-34 1	30-34 2	35-39 1	35-39 2	40-44 1	40-44 2	45-49 1	45-49 2	50-54 1	50-54 2	Total 20-54 1	Total 20-54 2
6	—	—	—	—	—	—	4	—	5	—	4 (1)	—	4 (2)	—	17 (3)	—
5	—	—	—	—	—	—	9	5	13 (3)	5 (1)	8 (5)	—	5 (2)	—	35 (10)	10 (1)
4	—	—	—	—	10	10	25 (5)	15 (2)	15 (7)	10 (4)	10 (7)	5 (4)	5 (11)	—	65 (30)	40 (10)
3	—	—	15	15	30	25	50 (10)	30 (8)	35 (15)	10 (6)	15 (10)	— (6)	10 (15)	—	155 (50)	80 (20)
2	5	5	40	40	45 (10)	35	— (25)	— (10)	— (30)	— (10)	— (15)	— (5)	— (10)	—	90 (90)	80 (35)
1	10	10	20	20	15 (10)	5 (5)	— (30)	— (10)	— (20)	— (10)	— (30)	— (10)	— (10)	—	45 (100)	35 (35)
TR	55	55	15	15	—	—	—	—	—	—	—	—	—	—	70	70
Totals	70	—	90	—	100 (20)	75 (15)	88 (70)	50 (30)	68 (75)	25 (31)	37 (68)	5 (25)	24 (50)	—	477 (283)	315 (101)

* "1" indicates number of men deemed promotable one level; "2" indicates number of men deemed promotable two levels, including men designated as being promotable one level.

NOTE: Figures in parentheses indicate men without a college education. TR = Trainees.

neers and scientists if these men are not considered to have cross-occupational promotion potential.)

STAFFING OF FUTURE POSITIONS

In order to determine what manpower will be utilized to staff future positions at various levels in the organization, a Replacement Development Table is constructed (Table 4-13). This table is designed to indicate the current resources of the organization with respect to future needs and the management development work that must be undertaken to provide enough manpower for future promotions.

The table contains information on the current college manpower under age 55 that is expected to be available in ten years. (A similiar table can be designed for non-college manpower.) The personnel are shown by current age, level, and promotability. The expanded column designations are as follows:

Column *a*: Total current manpower (expected to be available in ten years).

Column *b*: Current manpower rated non-promotable.

Column *c*: Current manpower rated promotable one level.

Column *d*: Current manpower rated promotable two levels.

Column *e*: Expected manpower requirements in year ten.

Columns *f* through *n* correspond to the organizational level indicated in the heading just below the column letter symbol (for example, column *f* corresponds to Level 9). The sums of the numbers in columns *f* through *n* indicate the year-ten forecasts of manpower by level. The numbers in each column indicate the manpower that will be drawn upon by various levels to fill the forecast positions, based on manpower expected to be available and promotable.

Construction of the table is as follows:

1. In Column *a*, the number of men who will be available at the end of year ten is entered by level. These numbers correspond to the figures developed earlier in Table 4-2.

2. For each level, men rated non-promotable (column *b*); promotable one level (column *c*); and promotable two levels

TABLE 4-13

REPLACEMENT DEVELOPMENT TABLE FOR COLLEGE GRADUATES – COMPANY Y

Level	Anticipated Manpower Resources				e Total Needed	Anticipated Positions That Must Be Filled in Year Ten								
	a Available	b Non-promotable	c Level Promotable 1	d 2		f 9	g 8	h 7	i 6	j 5	k 4	l 3	m 2	n 1 TR
9	—	—	—	—	1	—	—	—	—	—	—	—	—	—
8	3	—	3	—	8	1	2	—	—	—	—	—	—	—
7	17	—	17	—	45	—	6	11	—	—	—	—	—	—
6	35	25	10	—	115	—	—	10	25	—	—	—	—	—
5	50	25	25	7	160	—	—	7	18	25	—	—	—	—
4	80	20	60	35	205	—	—	—	35	25	20	—	—	—
3	155	25	130	65	110	—	—	—	—	65	65	25	—	—
2	75	—	75	70	115	—	—	—	—	—	70	5	—	—
1	30	—	30	30	40	—	—	—	—	—	—	30	—	—
TR	55	—	55	55	35	—	—	—	—	—	—	55	—	—
Total Positions	500	95	405	262	834	1	8	45	115	160	205	110	115	75
Current View of Replacement Deficiencies					334	—	—	17	37	45	50	(5)	115	75

(column d) are entered. Men promotable two levels are shown in both column c and column d.

3. The forecast number of positions in year ten is entered in column e.

4. The number of non-promotable men (from column b) is entered by level in the corresponding level column (columns f through n). For example, the 20 non-promotable men at level 4 are entered in column k which corresponds to Level 4.

5. Beginning with Level 9, the number of vacancies that must be filled at any level (indicated in column e) is determined. If incumbents at that level are insufficient to fill the positions, the number promotable from the next level down (from column c) is entered to complete the staffing needs of the level under analysis.

6. If promotable manpower is insufficient from the next level down, the number rated promotable two levels from the second level down is drawn upon to finish the staffing needs of the positions (from column d).

7. If promotable manpower is still insufficient, staffing of these positions must be made by persons not currently identified as having potential for the positions. This number is shown as the "Current view of replacement deficiencies" at the bottom of the table.

To illustrate this procedure, the staffing of Level 6 (column i) is described.

1. Of the 115 positions at Level 6, 25 will be filled by non-promotable men (from column b). The other 10 men currently in Level 6 are marked for promotion to Level 7 and thus cannot be used for Level 6 staffing.

2. Of the current Level 5 manpower, 25 are non-promotable; seven men with two-level promotion potential are designated for Level 7 jobs. This leaves 18 men for Level 6 staffing. They are entered in column i opposite Level 5 to indicate their source.

3. To complete the Level 6 staffing, manpower from Level 4 is required. Seventy-two Level 6 positions must still be filled. Only 35 men at Level 4 are now rated to have this potential. They are entered in column i opposite Level 4 to indicate their source.

4. Of the 115 projected Level 6 positions, current talent is

capable of filling 78 positions. This leaves 37 vacancies. They must be filled by talent either not now available or by lower management men with very high potential.

MANPOWER PROBLEMS

An interpretation of the Replacement Development Table reveals the following situations: The company currently lacks men to fill 17 top management (Level 7) positions. The Promotion Potential Table (Table 4-12) shows that ten men at Level 4 have apparent top management potential based on their career performance thus far. The manpower planner must examine these men individually to determine if this potential does really exist and if they can be developed in ten years for top management jobs. The loss analysis included provision for the attrition of seven men from Level 6 with promotion potential for Level 7. If this loss can be reduced, and if the company can arrange transfers of men with promotion potential from the parent company at Level 5 and Level 6, it should be able to meet the replacement challenge.

The table shows a need for immediate action in obtaining and developing high quality talent for future top management requirements. The situation in individual departments may compound the problem. Not all the men rated promotable to top management may have the necessary experience for specific top management vacancies. This may mean that new job assignments are required to prepare such men with top management potential for such specific top management jobs.

Similar demands on the organization exist at other levels. The analysis indicates that 45 positions at Level 5 may have to be filled by men now at Level 2. Due to recent rapid promotions of lower level manpower, some of the Level 2 men may already lack experience and knowledge of operating problems. Further rapid advancement might mean they will not be properly prepared for Level 5 positions.

If talent from the parent organization cannot be used to help meet the replacement problems, the company may wish to hire experienced manpower from outside. This manpower would be used in activities where shortages would be felt most keenly or where experience is vital to good performance.

Perhaps the greatest challenge facing Company Y, however, is in the non-college-trained management area. The manpower study indicates that 675 non-college men should be found for management in the next ten years. Previous hiring patterns indicate a probable shortage of men in the 35- to 44-year age group. The forecast of a smaller hourly wage group means that the opportunity to hire non-college men for eventual promotion to management is somewhat limited. A search among hourly personnel for men with managerial ability and their subsequent training and development are necessary to meet this problem. New selection standards for hourly personnel hiring should include the goal of identifying men with potential for promotion to management because of long-range management needs.

Another approach to the problem is to identify positions which might be filled by females. If the company is willing to experience a higher loss rate among new college hires, female college graduates could be used to fill some of the positions. As the number of college graduates at lower management increases, however, the promotion opportunities available to women diminish and turnover tends to rise.

Analysis of this type helps to reveal management manpower needs and potential problem areas that a manpower forecast alone does not show. An understanding of the relation of the current structure to the future structure enables the manpower planner to design action programs that will better serve the needs of the organization.

CONCLUSION – ACTION PROGRAM IMPLICATIONS

What might be done by Company Y to meet some of its manpower challenges? In addition to the earlier suggestions, Company Y could investigate the following items:

1. Can the voluntary separation rate, particularly among the men with high potential, be reduced?

2. Can management development problems be eased by reducing the probable middle management vacancies through retention of some men past their normal retirement dates?

3. Do all current middle management positions identified as requiring college educations really require this level of education?

4. Can transfers from the parent organization be reduced to help relieve the replacement problems?

5. How many men with management potential are available in the hourly ranks?

6. What changes in organization design can be made to reduce the future need for middle managers?

7. Can jobs be identified which develop younger men at a faster rate?

8. Can the company hire men from the outside without damaging the policy of promotion from within?

9. Are current estimates of promotion potential accurate, or has qualified manpower been overlooked?

10. Can men currently regarded as non-promotable be given training assignments that will make them promotable?

11. Can incentive systems be devised to increase management productivity, and thus help reduce the number of managers needed in the future?

Other questions can be asked about the manpower situation in Company Y. As indicated earlier, the data used are hypothetical, but the manpower relationships which are developed are similar to those that have been experienced in companies in the United States.

An examination of the type undertaken for Company Y provides insights into the management structure of an organization and how it behaves over time. This kind of information is useful to the manpower planner who is interested in helping his organization make the transition from its current manpower situation to its future circumstances. Awareness of the overall needs of the organization enables him to study the situations of individual managers in the organization. He is then able to design actions for specific individuals that make sense in terms of the overall organizational needs.

CHAPTER 5

THE MEASUREMENT OF LABOR
PRODUCTIVITY

The manpower planner should understand the nature of labor productivity and how it is measured. This understanding enables him to discuss the performance of the workforce more intelligently and provides empirical support for his recommendations in the manpower area.

Manpower forecasting is in an initial stage of development for most organizations. Only a relatively few companies have had much experience with the activity; many other companies involved in manpower planning on a limited basis make only modest attempts to forecast their future needs. The lack of agressive forecasting appears to be a result of a lack of knowledge of how to forecast. In this chapter and the next, an approach to manpower forecasting is developed. The analytical techniques and measurement processes provide a base for further refinements in the forecasting process. These refinements, however, are not treated in this book. They involve the use of statistical techniques such as correlation analysis of historical data and subjective probabilities regarding future possible events.

The forecasting method to be examined here relies on an analysis of labor productivity and the use of this information to estimate manpower. Although the primary concern is with managerial manpower, all manpower in the organization is considered because managerial manpower requirements relate directly to total manpower. In addition, an understanding of total manpower needs enables the planner to examine the relationship of his forecast with company financial forecasts. This examination will indicate how the labor costs of the manpower forecast relate to the profit plans of the firm.

Measurement of labor productivity does not require special training in economics or statistics. The techniques employed in the following analysis are basically arithmetical in nature. (Some of the refinements in the process are discussed in the appendix to the chapter. The use of labor productivity data in the actual manpower forecasting process is presented in Chapter 6.) Before discussing how to measure labor productivity, however, a brief summary of the measurement process and the manpower forecasting method is worth-while.

THE BASIC FORECASTING PROCEDURE

The production process of the company may be seen as that shown in Figure 5-1. Materials and supplies are processed by men, machines, and purchased services. These efforts result in goods and services which are distributed and sold to pay for production expenses and to provide profits as a return to investor capital.

Improvements in the production process may result in higher than "normal" profits. These may eventually give rise to higher wages, bonuses, dividends, or taxes. These "surplus" profits may also provide a stimulus for the purchase of new equipment, for additional research and development, or for some other expenditure.

The efficiency of the production process changes over time. As the quality of labor improves through better selection and training, the conversion of materials and supplies to goods and services can be expected to become more efficient (other factors remaining constant). More noticeable is the increase in efficiency which results when additional plant facilities and equipment are used in the production process. Efficiency changes also result when improvements take place in materials, supplies, and services.

In productivity studies, the concern is with determining the relationship of the input factors to the volume of output. The ratio developed by dividing input into output is the productivity level for that input. The rate at which this ratio changes over time is called the productivity rate for the input. Productivity, then, is the term used to describe efficiency in the production process — the output generated by a given unit of input.

FIGURE 5-1

THE PRODUCTION PROCESS OF THE FIRM

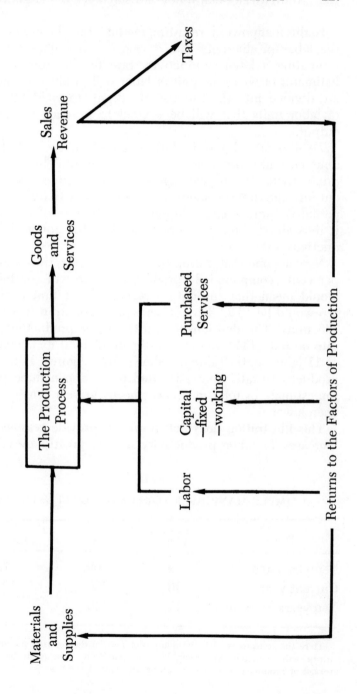

In this manpower forecasting method, the planner determines the labor productivity rate during the recent past to aid in estimating a labor productivity rate for the forecast period. Estimates of what one unit of labor will produce in the future are divided into the forecast of output, to yield the number of labor units that will be needed to produce the projected output.

To illustrate this procedure assume that each of the labor units currently produces ten units of output. This is the labor productivity. If ten years ago each unit produced 7.7 units of output, the improvement in labor productivity during the period is approximately 30 per cent. The rate of improvement is thus about three per cent annually — the annual labor productivity rate.

Now assume that during the next ten years, the annual three per cent [compounded] productivity rate will continue. This would mean that the output of each labor unit during year ten would be 13.2.[1] The estimate of total output in year ten is 145 units. The division of year-ten labor productivity (13.2) into output (145) yields an estimate of total manpower needs of 11 labor units. Table 5-1 shows these figures. If the annual productivity rate were estimated to be above three per cent, the estimate of total manpower needs in year ten would have been lower.

This illustration does not, however, provide reasons for the increases in labor productivity and it greatly oversimplifies

TABLE 5-1

A SIMPLE MANPOWER FORECASTING ILLUSTRATION

Year	Labor Units	Output Units	Output per Unit of Labor Input
Ten years ago	9	69	7.7
Current year	10	100	10.0
Ten years in future	11	145	13.2

[1] Here the concern is with the manpower needed *during* year ten because the output will be produced throughout the year. The forecast is based on the average of productivity at the beginning and end of the year.

some manpower forecasting problems. What, for example, is an appropriate measure of output? How are labor inputs measured?

LABOR PRODUCTIVITY

A major characteristic in Table 5-1 is the total emphasis on the labor factors of production. The illustration suggests that all the productivity gains in the company are the result of labor efforts. Whenever input is defined as only one of the production factors (e.g., labor), by definition all productivity gains are attributed to that unit.

Improved labor services do contribute to increases in overall company productivity, but the use of more capital, especially in plant and equipment, is another major factor in the process — if not the most important factor. This means that the use of capital in the production process is a concern of the manpower planner. Methods of analyzing the contribution of capital to company productivity are available.[2] (The appendix contains a brief discussion of these techniques. The role of fixed capital inputs in the manpower forecasting process is given treatment in Chapter 7.) The emphasis of this book on labor productivity is because of its key role in estimating future labor requirements.

To assist in the development of the discussion, output and input data from an American manufacturing company are presented. These data have been modified in some instances to provide greater clarity to the discussion and should not be viewed as pure empirical findings. It will also be seen that some useful cost information was not available to the analyst because of the accounting conventions used in the company. Where this occurs it is mentioned in the discussion.

MEASURING COMPANY OUTPUT

It has been seen that the analysis of productivity rests on a

---

[2] John W. Kendrick and Daniel Creamer, *Measuring Company Productivity; Handbook With Case Studies,* The Conference Board, Studies in Business Economics No. 89 (New York: National Industrial Conference Board, Inc., 1965). Those interested in the measurement of company productivity will find this monograph an extremely valuable reference. It contains careful explanations of many productivity measurement problems and examples of productivity studies in American companies. The discussions in this chapter and the appendix are greatly influenced by this monograph.

determination of the relationship between output and input. One of the first tasks of the analyst, then, is to determine how to measure the output of the organization.

The major criterion to use in the selection of which output unit to measure is that it must be causally related to the input units. For an organization which sells its output, the dollar value of its goods and services is an appropriate measure of output. For government, educational, military and similiar types of institutions, a dollar value for services is not available. For most activities inside a company, a dollar value does not exist for production efforts, except perhaps where profit or cost centers exist.

When there is no dollar value to measure output, a physical unit of measurement is used. Vouchers processed or customers served are typical units. Determination of appropriate physical output units may be difficult. The unit selected should respond to changes in labor inputs, and labor requirements should change as the volume of the output units changes. In addition, the relationship should be useful over time. In other words, the output selected is not one which the firm will cease producing in the near future, or one that will become only a minor part of its activities.

A problem with using physical units as the output measure for the company as a whole arises because of frequent changes in the product mix of the company. Table 5-2 shows the product line history of the Midwest Company for a ten-year period.[3]

At the end of the ten-year period, only two products produced in year one were still being manufactured. And both of these items had changed in design, quality, and price. These figures reveal a typical difficulty in using physical units as the output units. The firm might produce a new item this year in twice the volume of an item discontinued from last year, yet the labor required to produce either product might be the same.

Selection of dollar values as the output units helps overcome

---

[3] At the time of this study, the Midwest Company employed about 900 workers. Its operations were in a single plant and it had line and staff activities. Products were consumer goods ranging in retail price from $15 to $100. Distribution was through wholesalers, retailers, and discount houses. The industry is very competitive and in recent years a high rate of product innovation has occurred.

TABLE 5-2

PRODUCT LINE HISTORY — MIDWEST COMPANY

Year	Products Discontinued During Previous Year	Products Introduced During the Year	Total Items in Product Line
1	1	1	14
2	3	1	12
3	5	3	10
4	1	4	13
5	0	3	16
6	2	6	20
7	1	7	26
8	3	8	31
9	5	10	36
10	4	11	43

such problems. In addition, the ability to relate manpower estimates to the company's profit plans increases when dollars are used as the output units. Sales revenue quickly comes to mind as a way to measure output. Its major advantage is that it is easy to understand and measure; but, unfortunately, it is often a very misleading measure of output. One reason it is inadequate is because of inventory changes. When inventories are increased labor inputs are used which do not appear in sales revenue. When inventories are decreased, sales revenues reflect production efforts of previous periods. Another problem with sales revenue results from the nature of a firm's purchases. These purchases represent the production efforts of other companies and not of that being studied. A company may decide to make something it has been purchasing. Sales revenue may remain the same, but the labor force will have to increase to produce these products. In addition, if the firm must pay higher prices for materials, it may raise its own prices. This means added sales revenue without use of additional labor.

VALUE ADDED

To avoid these difficulties with sales revenue, the economist's concept of real "value added" is used to measure output. Value added is the market value of the goods and services after subtracting purchases for intermediate goods and services.

Sales revenue is reduced by the purchase costs of the materials, supplies, and services used in the firm's production process. (Major service items include marketing and distribution expenses for advertising and transportation.) This process yields that portion of sales revenue that the company "adds to the value" of the products and services it sells. The use of the word "real" in association with "value added," means that the values are in constant dollar terms. That is, the value added for any year is not influenced by price changes. Dollar values used for each year in the study are common to the one year that has been selected to serve as the base year for prices.

Five computation steps are required to determine value added. Data from the Midwest Company are given to show how each step affects output measurement.

Step 1. Adjust sales for inventory changes. Final sales revenue for each year is adjusted for changes in finished goods inventories and work-in-process inventories. Any increase in these inventories is added to the sales total, and any decrease subtracted. This results in a value for the products made each year, not for the products sold during that year. If possible, the finished goods inventory is valued at market prices, so that it more closely approximates sales revenue. The work-in-process inventory may have to be valued at cost because of the difficulty of assigning a market value to partially completed goods.

Step 2. Adjust sales revenue for price changes. The revised sales figure is now adjusted to reflect changes in product prices during the period, through a price deflator to make sales comparable with one another in constant dollar terms. A deflator may be constructed from company sales and price records or from a price index published by the government. (A discussion of price indices is included in the chapter appendix.) Table 5-4 shows the effect of the price adjustment on the Midwest Company's revenue figures. The price deflator used was constructed from company records.

Step 3. Adjust purchases for inventory changes. Individual year purchases are now adjusted for changes in inventory. Decreases in the materials inventory are added to the total purchase costs of materials and supplies. Increases in the in-

TABLE 5-3

MIDWEST COMPANY SALES ADJUSTED FOR
INVENTORY CHANGES
(In Thousands)

Year	Sales	Inventory Changes*	Sales Adjusted for Inventory Change
1	$ 9,699	+$1,342	$11,041
2	17,066	+ 299	17,365
3	22,375	+ 1,086	23,461
4	22,971	− 1,122	21,849
5	22,141	− 929	21,212
6	21,436	+ 216	21,652
7	20,211	+ 844	21,055
8	20,501	+ 134	20,635
9	20,202	+ 105	20,307
10	21,044	+ 462	21,506

* All inventories valued at cost.

TABLE 5-4

MIDWEST COMPANY SALES ADJUSTED FOR PRICE CHANGES
(In Thousands)

Year	Inventory Adjusted Sales Revenue	Company Price Index	Price Adjusted Revenue
1	$11,041	100.0	$11,041
2	17,365	104.2	16,665
3	23,461	105.8	22,175
4	21,849	105.6	20,690
5	21,212	104.5	20,299
6	21,652	104.2	20,779
7	21,055	106.8	19,714
8	20,635	98.6	20,928
9	20,307	92.7	21,906
10	21,506	93.0	23,125

ventory are subtracted from the purchase total. The resulting final net figure reflects only the use of materials and supplies during the year, not their purchase prices.

Step 4. Adjust purchases for price changes. The materials and supplies are next adjusted for changes in prices of these items. Since construction of a company price deflator for purchases is difficult because of the wide variety of purchases and a frequent lack of necessary data, government wholesale price indices are often useful in this step. The value of purchased services is similiarly adjusted for changes in price level.

In the Midwest Company, a Bureau of Labor Statistics intermediate goods wholesale price index was used to adjust purchase costs of materials, supplies, and services. Included in these purchases were goods bought and resold without further manufacturing effort, contract work, fuel and electricity, and such distribution expenses as advertising and transportation. When the company transferred from a fiscal-year reporting system to a year-end reporting system midway through the study period, monthly figures permitted the reconcilation of most expenses to a calendar-year basis, although for some items, such as depreciation, this was not possible.

Step 5. Subtract adjusted purchases from adjusted revenue. Value added is now obtained by subtracting the value of purchases from the adjusted revenue figure. As indicated earlier, these include the inventory and price-adjusted totals for purchases of materials, supplies, and services. Rent, depreciation, and indirect business taxes are also deducted to determine the "net" value-added total. If rent, depreciation, and indirect business taxes are not deducted in this step, the value-added total is a "gross" figure. (These considerations are elaborated upon in the appendix.) In the Midwest Company, the change in the accounting period did not permit the deduction of these items, and thus a gross value-added figure was used in the productivity study. Table 5-6 shows these data for the Midwest Company.

The difference in the valuation of output for the Midwest Company between the value-added method and sales-revenue method is shown in Table 5-7, which is a series of index numbers for the different output totals of the company. They indi-

TABLE 5-5

MIDWEST COMPANY PURCHASES ADJUSTED FOR INVENTORY AND PRICE CHANGES

Year	Purchases*	Inventory Adjustments	Price† Index	Adjusted Purchases
1	$ 4,441	$ 4,429	100.0	$ 4,429
2	7,353	7,357	97.1	7,577
3	11,884	11,894	97.6	12,186
4	10,096	10,083	98.2	10,268
5	9,536	9,437	100.1	9,428
6	10,747	10,770	104.5	10,306
7	10,655	10,698	107.0	9,998
8	11,332	11,398	107.1	10,642
9	12,261	12,050	108.9	11,065
10	12,180	12,223	108.7	11,245

* Purchases include items bought and resold without further manufacturing effort: fuel, electricity, contract work, and services such as transportation and advertising.

† Price index from the Bureau of Labor Statistics for intermediate goods at the wholesale level.

TABLE 5-6

MIDWEST COMPANY GROSS VALUE ADDED
(In Thousands)

Year	Adjusted Revenue	Adjusted Purchases	Value Added
1	$11,041	$ 4,429	$ 6,612
2	16,665	7,577	9,088
3	22,175	12,186	9,989
4	20,690	10,268	10,422
5	20,299	9,428	10,871
6	20,779	10,306	10,473
7	19,714	9,998	9,716
8	22,956	10,642	10,286
9	21,906	11,065	10,841
10	23,125	11,245	11,880

cate that the production effort may be interpreted quite differently, depending upon how output is measured. The value-added series indicates that the last three years were high production years in terms of the real contribution by the company to the products sold. The sales-revenue data on the other hand indicate that these years were at best only average output years in comparison with earlier years of the sales-revenue series.

To determine the real output of labor the value-added method was used. Although it is not as easy to determine as sales-revenue or inventory-adjusted revenue, it relates much more functionally to the productivity of labor inputs. In attempting to forecast manpower, the concern is with the output labor produces. To attribute (or neglect to attribute) to labor, output values that arise because of inventory, price, or make-versus-buy decision changes is not desirable.

TABLE 5-7
MIDWEST COMPANY OUTPUT INDICES

Year	Sales Revenue	Inventory Adjusted Revenue	Price and Inventory Adjusted Revenue	Gross Value Added
1	100	100	100	100
2	176	157	151	137
3	231	212	201	151
4	237	198	187	158
5	228	192	184	164
6	221	196	188	158
7	208	191	179	147
8	211	205	208	156
9	208	184	198	164
10	202	195	209	180

MEASURING LABOR INPUT

Fewer problems exist in measuring labor input than in measuring output. Problems do exist, however, which are elaborated upon in the appendix. To measure labor input, there is a choice of three units: actual man-hours worked, average annual employment, or total wages paid. When the primary concern is with forecasting future managerial employment, average annual employment serves as a suitable input unit.

Wages paid, as a labor input unit are, however, also important in manpower forecasting. The concern over what a labor dollar generates in adding value is especially important in managerial decision-making. Man-hour productivity may be improving, for example, but at the same time labor dollar productivity may be declining because of rising wages. Further, because the planner wishes to determine the relationship of his manpower forecast to the profit plan, he needs an estimate of the total wage bill of the manpower forecast. Historical information on labor dollar productivity is, again, helpful.

In using wage and salary data in productivity studies, it is necessary to adjust the data for changes in total labor expenses that result from higher wage rates rather than from the use of additional labor. This adjustment is made by a wage deflator, just as sales revenue is adjusted by a price deflator. The wage pattern of each company has its individual characteristics. For this reason a wage deflator must be constructed from company data. Indices of wages published by government for a particular industry or region usually will not reflect characteristics of any one company.

When these adjustments are made at least two deflators should be used. One is used for hourly employees, and the other for salaried personnel, because the changes in the wage structure for these two groups do not occur in the same manner. Overtime wages and changes in the size of the salaried group, for example, can alter the average wage of employees in these classifications significantly. It may be desirable to use additional deflators to adjust wages for salaried-exempt and nonexempt personnel or for any other payroll group considered significant. (A description of how to construct these deflators is contained in the appendix.)

Table 5-8 shows the labor input of the Midwest Company. Average annual employment is based on a 13-month average of ending monthly employment.[4] Adjusted wages and salaries

---

[4] This enables the planner to obtain an average yearly employment figure which includes both year-end and first-of-year employment levels. He uses the end of December employment total from the previous year to represent the January 1 level for the year under study.

are based on separate wage deflators for the hourly and salaried payroll groups. The base period for these deflators is the first year of the study period.

TABLE 5-8

MIDWEST COMPANY LABOR INPUT UTILIZATION
(Wages in Thousands)

Year	Average Annual Employment	Adjusted Total Wages
1	777	$3,291
2	1045	4,386
3	1123	4,814
4	1121	4,684
5	1048	4,442
6	1005	4,221
7	897	3,802
8	895	3,801
9	871	3,863
10	897	3,935

MEASURING LABOR PRODUCTIVITY

The determination of labor productivity is now undertaken by dividing value added for each year by the corresponding labor input. The productivity of the Midwest Company is shown in Table 5-9. The value-added totals are from Table 5-6; the labor input totals from Table 5-8.

Determination of the productivity of labor in each year of the historical analysis permits examination of the pattern of productivity change during the period. This knowledge is helpful when a productivity rate is selected for use in estimating future labor productivity levels. Lack of year-to-year data reduces ability to select a rate for the future. In the illustration of a simple manpower forecasting procedure given at the beginning of the chapter, the average annual productivity rate for the historical period was all that was known. This rate might have been the result of some quite widely varying pat-

TABLE 5-9
MIDWEST COMPANY LABOR PRODUCTIVITY

Year	Output per Employee	Output per Constant Labor Dollar
1	$ 8,510	$2.01
2	8,697	2.07
3	8,895	2.08
4	9,297	2.23
5	10,373	2.45
6	10,421	2.48
7	10,832	2.55
8	11,493	2.71
9	12,447	2.81
10	13,244	3.02

terns of productivity growth during the period. The selection of a three per cent rate for the future might then have been a poor decision.

CONCLUSION

Labor productivity measurement requires a large amount of effort when first undertaken. A lack of relevant information and changes in accounting conventions may complicate the collection and analysis of historical data, as was the situation with the Midwest Company.

After the initial historical analysis, the productivity study effort becomes much easier. Subsequent studies require an updating of the data for the production efforts of the previous year. Refinements of the earlier analysis may be undertaken as the forecaster gains experience in productivity measurement.

If economic or statistical researchers are available in the organization, they may be called upon to perform the analysis. If this support is not available, use of a staff personnel manager to make the analysis is probably required. The information generated by the study is worth the cost of making it. Requests for information on the nature of the company price and wage indexes, its value added, and its productivity may prompt interest and use of the information by others in the company in their managerial decision-making capacities.

The manpower planner should understand the nature of labor productivity and how it is measured. This understanding enables him to discuss the performance of the workforce more intelligently and provides empirical support for his recommendations in the manpower area. The data can provide guidance on wage and price change decisions. They help demonstrate the need for labor cost consciousness. They may reveal the need for the addition of certain kinds of persons (e.g., industrial engineers and systems specialists) whose task is to effect cost reductions and improve general efficiency. If the manpower planner is not able to discuss labor productivity with other planners and top management, he may discover that some other person in the organization is doing it for him. When this happens, his influence on manpower matters is lessened.

SPECIAL PROBLEMS IN PRODUCTIVITY MEASUREMENT

Several considerations in labor productivity measurement were not discussed in Chapter 5. The measurement task is complicated because special procedures are required to overcome certain problems. Examination of these considerations is undertaken in this appendix.

THE BASIC FORECASTING PROCEDURE

An implicit assumption in the manpower forecasting method discussed in Chapter 5 is that the major determinant of output over a long time period is the demand for goods and services. Economic theory tends to focus on short-run periods and emphasizes that the output level is a function of the number of input factors used. In the long run, a shortage of capital may result in output that is less than demand. But long-range financial projections have as an objective the elimination of these output restraints by an early determination of capital requirements. Long-range manpower forecasting has the same basic objective — that of insuring that the company has adequate manpower to meet future demands for its goods and services. The concern is primarily with the "high talent" or salaried-exempt employee who requires a long lead time for recruitment and development.

OTHER PRODUCTIVITY MEASUREMENTS

Because labor productivity studies result in the measurement of the labor factor of production only, all productivity gains are attributed to labor. In general, when labor productivity increases, labor does not expend additional energy. The majority of labor productivity improvements result from management's decisions to substitute plant and equipment for labor. Thus, success and failure in labor productivity gains are the results of the quality of managerial decisions.

The measurement of other production factors in productivity analysis is undertaken in the total-productivity approach. In this procedure, the combined values of labor, capital, and the goods and services used in the production process are the input values in the study. These are divided into sales revenue that is adjusted for inventory and price changes. Because intermediate goods and services are part of the input values, they are not deducted from sales revenue. Value added is thus not used in this method.

Another productivity measurement is total-factor productivity. This approach is informative in manpower forecasting because the contribution of capital to productivity is determined. Real net value added is divided by the combined amount of capital and labor used to produce it in order to determine total factor productivity. A full discussion of this technique is provided by Kendrick and Creamer in their monograph, with a case illustration from a large manufacturing company.[1] In their discussion, the rather difficult problem of measuring capital input is treated in some detail. Essentially they recommend determining the value of all capital (not just fixed assets) used during the production period. This is converted to a constant dollar basis through appropriate price indexes. The base period rate of return on investment plus all interest charges is then divided by this capital investment to obtain capital input for the period.

The most difficult problem in the process is to obtain an accurate valuation of capital investment. Different price indices for the different types of capital used, recognition of depreciation conventions, and the valuation of land may complicate the process. Kendrick and Creamer do not appear to express a preference as to whether capital goods should be measured in gross terms or in net of depreciation. In the case studies cited, gross valuation is used.

VALUE ADDED

Subtracting goods and services purchases and indirect business taxes from sales revenue results in a value-added figure.

---

[1] Kendrick and Creamer, *op. cit.*

Included in purchases are depreciation charges and rental expenses. Depreciation is considered a time payment for goods purchased from others. Rent is a payment for the use of facilities owned by others; it appears as part of their income and, to the extent it exceeds their own depreciation or amoritization charges, it is part of their value added. Indirect business taxes (i.e., taxes which are charged as business expenses) such as property taxes are not part of value added because they cannot be traced directly to government services received for the taxes. An exception is made for social security and other employee taxes, which are included in value added because they are considered part of the hiring cost of labor. These exclusions, on a constant dollar basis, result in "real net value added" for the company.

If depreciation, rent, and indirect business taxes are not netted from sales, the resulting figure is "real gross value added." This output value might be used because of a lack of historical information on these expenses, as was required in the Midwest Company example because of a lack of accounting data and of changes in accounting procedures.

The revenue figure used in the calculations of value added does not include dollars generated from activities not clearly related to the basic mission of the firm or to those only slightly related to labor usage. A company might earn revenue from short-term securities or rent from miscellaneous properties. These activities, for non-financial firms, are incidental to the basic mission. The revenue generated usually requires only slight labor input relative to the total mission. Furthermore, the activities may produce an uneven revenue stream over time (e.g., when properties are sold) and thus distort the output levels. When the activities are a significant portion of the mission and require a significant amount of labor for administration they should be included. Banks and insurance companies fit into this category.

Internal asset production. A make-versus-buy decision that is easily overlooked in output measurement involves the use of company manpower to build plant and equipment. The manpower used in this production is reflected in the labor input figures of the productivity study. The output of those efforts, however, is not reflected in sales revenue. This situation is typical of metal-working companies that manufacture much of their own equipment. It is also true of companies that maintain a construction labor pool for plant additions and modifications. Many electric power companies employed large numbers of engineers and skilled craftsmen for their post-World War II construction programs. The value of this type of effort should be added to the value added for the year. As in other output figures, the value should be adjusted for price changes. A Bureau of Labor Statistics price index for these goods is an appropriate index to use because the alternative to making is to purchase plant and equipment in the market.

Changes in product quality. Perhaps the most difficult aspect of output measurement involves changes in the quality of products produced. These quality changes may require added labor effort. When sales revenue is adjusted for price level changes there is a tendency to eliminate from the revenue total that portion generated by the added quality. Thus the labor productivity appears to be lower than it really should be. Kendrick and Creamer suggest several methods of coping with this problem.[2] These methods may become quite complicated and are subject to a variety of errors because subjective judgment is required. Because of these difficulties and the relatively small impact of these adjustments on the manpower forecast it appears that most manpower planners need not worry about the problem.

PRICE INDICES

Output is valued in constant dollars in order to determine the real change in the output/input relationship. Price indices are used to relate values in the productivity study to those that existed in a common base period. The index number of a given year is divided into the value of the items being adjusted to obtain the "real" value for the items.

Construction of a company price index has advantages over the use of government-published indices. Government indices reflect general market conditions for goods and services. They may not relate accurately to company conditions where a variety of price discounts and special market conditions may exist.

---

[2] *Ibid.*, pp. 25-28.

In addition, many of the government indices cover a variety of goods in a general product category. Price movements of the different goods are merged together into a single index. When the index contains items not produced by the company, it may not reflect the price behavior of the company products.

Table 5-10 shows a price index for the Midwest Company and the price index published by the Bureau of Labor Statistics for the product group which includes the products of the Midwest Company. The Consumer Price Index for the same years is also shown for comparison purposes.

TABLE 5-10
SELECTED PRICE INDICES

Year	Company Index	Consumer Price Index	Appropriate BLS* Price Index
1	100.0	100.0	100.0
2	104.2	103.3	103.2
3	105.8	104.1	93.2
4	105.6	104.5	97.7
5	104.5	104.2	87.7
6	104.2	105.7	86.7
7	106.8	109.4	85.5
8	98.6	112.3	89.8
9	92.7	114.3	90.1
10	93.0	115.2	87.8

* Bureau of Labor Statistics.

The figures indicate that the company price movements did not correspond very closely with the appropriate government index. The government index is a composite of a variety of items sold through particular types of retail outlets. Although the company did sell some of its products through these outlets, the majority of its sales were through other channels. The Consumer Price Index movements were quite close to those of the company through year six, but significant deviations in the two series appear after that point.

Because of product line changes, for most companies construction of a price index is a somewhat complicated process.

A statistical tool known as the "chain index" is available to help cope with this problem. Although not widely used in statistics, it is important in the construction of price indices. Numbers in this index relate rather well with one another, even though the components of each number are slightly different. Since in the chain index different products are included on a year-to-year basis, product line changes can be tolerated when comparing the price or cost structure of a group of products.[3]

The initial step in construction of the price index is to multiply the current price of a product by the quantity of that product sold in the previous year. (Products not produced in successive years are thus not included in the yearly totals.) The calculation indicates the value of the previous year's output in terms of current prices. The calculations made for each product are then combined to obtain a total value for the year. This revenue sum is then divided by the total revenue from the previous year. The percentage result is the price change for all the products in the index compared with the previous year's prices.

This number is related to the price level of the base year by multiplying it by the index number of the previous year. The result of this multiplication is the index number for the current year. In this way, the price level of each year is chained to the base year. For example, assume that year-three prices are 112 per cent of year two's, and year-two prices are 110 per cent of base year one's. The chain index would read:

Year 1   100.0   (Base year 100)
Year 2   110.0   (110.0 x 100.0)
Year 3   123.2   (112.0 x 110.0)

This procedure is followed for each succeeding year in the price series.

Although the chain-index number approach is subject to some imprecision, it does provide a means of dealing with changes in the product line. The method outlined here is somewhat different from those which use only quantities from a

---

[3] See Frederick E. Croxton and Dudley J. Cowden, *Applied General Statistics* (New York: Prentice Hall, 1939), Chapter 21. This chapter contains a thorough discussion of this index. Other statistical textbooks also may be consulted for information on chain-index number construction.

single base year against prices for each year of the series. When a new product is introduced into the series, it substitutes for a base year product. This is the procedure used in the addition and deletion of products used for the Consumer Price Index.

MEASURING LABOR INPUTS

The problems relating to the three types of labor input units that can be used in productivity studies are discussed below.

Average Annual Employment

Average annual employment may not accurately reflect the actual manpower utilized during a production period, because changes in the use of overtime and short work weeks do not appear in annual employment statistics. Further, changes in vacations, holidays, and other forms of time off do not appear in these statistics and thus it is possible for average employment to increase during a year, while actual labor inputs remain constant or decrease. Average annual employment statistics may have to be adjusted when significant yearly differences occur in these factors.

Actual Man-hours Worked

Because of the problems with average annual employment data, economists tend to prefer to use actual man-hours worked as the manpower input unit. These figures reflect overtime usage and time lost due to vacations, sickness, holidays, and other reasons. Actual man-hours worked differ from compensated man-hours because of the hours that are paid for but not worked by the latter criterion. Imputations for man-hours of salaried employees usually are required because of a lack of man-hour data on these personnel.[4] Overtime hours are available for salaried non-exempt employees from payroll records, but usually have to be estimated for exempt employees. Man-hours are converted into employees by dividing the total man-hour figure by the average annual man-hours worked per person.

Changes in the quality of the workforce, however, are not reflected by man-hour figures. Higher quality labor should pro-

---

[4]If the average salaried work-week is 40 hours, the potential work-year is 2,080 man-hours. This sum would be reduced to 1,880 if the average time off per employee is 25 days.

duce more output than lower quality labor, but man-hours do not reflect this. By weighting higher quality labor-hours that are substituted for lower quality labor-hours by base period wages this distortion is offset. These adjustments are made for major occupational groups in the workforce.[5]

Most government labor productivity figures are in man-hour terms. The government-suggested 3.2 per cent labor productivity wage and price guidelines are based on output per man-hour. As salaried employment grows, man-hour imputations for these persons will increase. For this reason, manpower planners who use man-hours in productivity studies probably will need to establish an information system that reports actual salaried man-hours worked.

Wages and Salaries Paid

Labor dollars as the labor input units are relatively easy to determine from payroll records. In addition, payroll data are usually available for the various occupational groups (e.g., engineering, technical, etc.), wage groups, and for organizational units. The easy uniform identification of input by different personnel components through use of wage data is one of the principal advantages of this approach.

Disadvantages arise in using labor dollars, nevertheless. Wages are paid for time that is not worked, and thus generate productivity data that are not clearly related to physical input units such as man-hours. For manpower planning purposes, however, this difficulty is not a serious problem because the manpower planner is concerned with the amount of output generated by all labor expenses.

More troublesome is the fact that the wage bill increases without any increase in the amount of physical labor used in production. As wages rise due to such factors as cost of living allowances and labor contract provisions, measured labor productivity falls. To make year-to-year productivity data comparable wage deflators are used. At least two wage deflators, one for hourly workers and one for salaried workers, are usually needed because in most instances wage increases vary considerably for these employment groups.

---

[5] For further information on this subject see Kendrick and Creamer, *op. cit.*, pp. 35-36.

A wage deflator is constructed by first obtaining the average employee hourly wage or salary for each year of the productivity study. The first year is taken as the base year and the value for each subsequent year is divided by the base year. The index numbers constitute the wage deflators, which are divided into total wages for the associated year to convert these wages to base period dollars.

When the planner uses deflated wages he avoids the problem encountered in using man-hours that arises from substitution of higher quality labor for lower quality labor. The more skilled workers are counted more heavily as input units because of their higher wages. Using separate wage deflators for various occupational or wage groups gives a clearer indication of the relative contribution of each group to total labor inputs and lessens the chance of over- or underadjusting for workforce quality changes.

THE LENGTH OF THE TIME PERIOD STUDIED

A final consideration in productivity analysis is the time period studied. The period should be sufficiently long to provide insights into labor productivity, with particular emphasis on current trends.

The availability of data may limit the historic length of the analysis. Major changes in operations may also restrict the length of the study. Movement into a new production facility, for example, may make the data of the former facility incomparable with data from new operations. The analysis becomes more difficult the farther back it extends. Changes in accounting and reporting systems will affect the data and complicate the identification of input and output units.

The use of moving averages to study productivity movements is facilitated if a large number of years are examined. (The use of these averages is shown in the next chapter.) Examining additional years permits the construction of additional averages and thus more data for estimating the future. It also permits construction of wider time intervals for the moving averages and thus greater smoothing of unusually high or low productivity years.

Finally, whenever the planner compares the growth in productivity, wages, or prices of any one year in the study to the original year of the study, he faces an important measurement problem. The percentage growth in year eight, for example, compared with year one may not provide a clear reflection of the events during the period because year one may not have been a representative, or normal, year. If it had been a year of depressed productivity, wages, or prices, the comparison would have shown an above-average growth by year eight. Conversely, if year one had been a year of unusually high productivity, wages, or prices, the comparison would understate the developments during the period to some extent. This means that whenever the planner wishes to compare results back to a base period, he must select the base year with care to insure that it is representative of that period in time. Frequently, it is advisable to average the results of a consecutive three-year period in order to establish a representative base year.

CHAPTER 6

MAKING A MANPOWER FORECAST

Facts and figures of industrial and commercial operations have been shouting warnings about future events. But as yet we have not fully learned the significance of these warnings. As we do learn the symbols in a mathematical and statistical scheme of communication and understand their meaning we will solve better the riddles of what the future holds.

— E. H. MacNiece

The manpower forecasting procedure involves estimating the labor required to produce future output. This is determined by projecting a labor productivity rate into the future to estimate the output the planner expects each unit of labor to produce. The productivity of a unit of labor is divided into the future output forecast to make a manpower estimate.

There is no method of forecasting future labor productivity with complete certainty. Annual updating of productivity data and examination of factors that might affect future labor productivity are the best means available to improve the quality of estimates.

Knowledge of the past labor productivity growth in the firm helps to estimate future growth. If it were found, for example, that the annual productivity growth during the past ten years stayed within a five to seven per cent range, if the company operates within a stable environment, and technological advances are not expected to differ significantly from the past, the planner may estimate that the past pattern will continue. Any erratic movements of the past growth in labor productivity make the estimation task much more difficult.

In addition to information on the past performance of labor, attempts should be made to determine how future conditions might differ from those in the past. New technology might increase the productivity rate, or a smaller productivity growth

151

might be anticipated in the forecast period because recent technological breakthroughs are unlikely to be repeated.

Of significance in this determination are the research and development activities of supplier firms for the firm's industry as well as its own research and development efforts. Major product improvements may be under development by producer goods manufacturers that will raise the productivity of firms that use such equipment. Improvements in the materials and supplies used may also increase productivity. The dollars spent on R & D work probably have their most profound effect on productivity several years after the expenditure. This means that the recent emphasis on research in this country may have yet to reveal its impact on our labor productivity.

The rate at which a company adds to its fixed capital is also very important in productivity estimations. The relationship between the past accumulation of fixed assets and labor productivity should be studied because the net fixed asset growth rate may bear a strong relationship to the labor productivity rate. If such a relationship exists, the planner can examine the projection of asset formation to estimate the impact the rate might have on future labor productivity gains.[1] Information on future capital investment is obtained from production managers, engineering personnel, capital budgeting experts, and others concerned with production efficiency.

FORECASTING LABOR PRODUCTIVITY

A helpful method for examining labor productivity growth is through the use of moving averages. In this technique the average growth in productivity is examined for certain time periods. If the planner is making a five-year manpower forecast, he can examine labor productivity changes in former five-year periods. Examination of the Midwest Company data shows how this is done. Table 6-1 is the year-to-year percentage change in labor productivity on the basis of output per employee.

---

[1] The use of moving averages in the time series relationships of fixed asset growth to labor productivity growth may be helpful in this analysis. This helps to reflect the impact of major plant improvements on labor productivity for more than the year in which the additions are introduced. The full influence of new fixed assets on labor productivity may not appear in the year of introduction due to the length of the break-in period.

The yearly percentage changes are now grouped by five-year periods. The Midwest Company data are shown in Table 6-2.

These figures indicate that the range of productivity increases for five-year periods was between 4.2 per cent and 6.1 per cent. The 11.6 per cent gain in productivity in year five and the 0.5 per cent gain in year six are smoothed out by the moving average technique.

TABLE 6-1

MIDWEST COMPANY ANNUAL LABOR PRODUCTIVITY
CHANGES
(Value Added ÷ Average Annual Employment)

Year	Percentage Change from Previous Year
2	2.2
3	2.3
4	4.5
5	11.6
6	0.5
7	3.9
8	6.1
9	8.3
10	6.4

TABLE 6-2

MIDWEST COMPANY FIVE-YEAR AVERAGES OF LABOR
PRODUCTIVITY CHANGES

Period	Five-year Average (Per Cent)
Years 2- 6	4.22
Years 3- 7	4.56
Years 4- 8	5.32
Years 5- 9	6.08
Years 6-10	5.04

The statistics for other time periods, their relationship to past efforts designed to improve efficiency (e.g., a new plant layout), and the use of new equipment (e.g., data-processing equipment in clerical operations) were examined. After discussions with production and finance officials regarding future investment plans, these considerations led to the conclusion that the future labor productivity rate could be expected to be an improvement over past rates. For planning purposes it was agreed that a seven per cent annual rate was the best estimate to make at the time of the forecast.

The seven per cent rate was applied to the current value added per employee, compounded both for five years and four years, and the average was taken to estimate average employment during the fifth year when the value added would be produced. The forecast used the current value added per employee on an inventory-adjusted basis but without price adjustments. This was because the forecast sales and value added were in terms of current prices and not the historical base-year prices used in the productivity analysis. Table 6-3 shows these figures.

TABLE 6-3

MIDWEST COMPANY LABOR PRODUCTIVITY FORECAST

Current Labor Productivity	Year Four (End) Productivity Forecast	Year Five (End) Productivity Forecast	Year Five (Average) Productivity Forecast
$10,349	$13,073	$13,877	$13,460

Sales of $27,600,000 (in current dollar terms) were forecast for year five. It was estimated that value added would be 50 per cent of sales. This estimate was based on an evaluation of the make-versus-buy trend, recent experience, and anticipation of future production decisions. This resulted in a value-added estimate of $13,800,000 for year five.[2]

[2] The manpower forecaster must ascertain whether the sales and value-added forecast is in current dollar terms or includes an allowance for price increases. If the sales and purchases forecasts are not in current dollar terms they should be adjusted to current dollars because the labor productivity estimate for the forecast year is in current dollars. An alternative is to adjust the labor productivity estimate to future dollar terms.

The estimated labor productivity per employee of $10,349 divided into the estimated value added of $13,800,000 yielded a workforce estimate of 985 employees. This is the manpower forecast for the average employment during year five. Table 6-4 shows these figures, with the current year values.

TABLE 6-4

MIDWEST COMPANY MANPOWER FORECAST
(Sales and Value Added in Thousands)

	Sales	Value Added	Value Added per Employee	Average Annual Employment
Current year	$21,500	$12,220	$10,349	897
Forecast year	27,600	13,800	14,044	985

The accuracy of the manpower forecast depends upon how accurate the estimates of sales, value added, and labor productivity prove to be. The forecast indicates that the projected 48 per cent increase in output will require an approximate 14 per cent increase in employment.[3]

RANGE FORECASTING

A final point estimate of expected manpower requirements must be made for detailed planning purposes. Range estimates, however, are useful to facilitate contingency planning over a possible range of manpower needs. Different assumptions regarding labor productivity and value added can be made

---

[3] When mergers or acquisitions are contemplated, a thorough study of the manpower implications of such decisions should be made. Emphasis is usually on the quality and quantity of corporate staff personnel, line managers, and research and engineering personnel. Numerous other aspect of manpower management must also be explored, such as the differences in wage and benefit plans and union contracts. See Clarence I. Drayton, Jr., Craig Emerson, and John D. Griswold, *Mergers and Acquisitions: Planning and Action* (New York: Financial Executives Research Foundation, 1963), pp. 25-26. Also, Myles L. Mace and George C. Montgomery, Jr., *Management Problems of Corporate Acquisitions* (Boston: Harvard University, 1962), and Thomas L. Whisler, "Organizational Aspects of Corporate Growth," in William W. Alberts and Joel E. Segall, *The Corporate Merger* (Chicago: University of Chicago Press, 1966).

to generate manpower estimates for these situations. The analyst may believe that his productivity estimate is prone to be more in error on one side than another, which will cause him to estimate a manpower range that varies more in one direction than the other around his point estimate.

Without forecasting experience on which to base error expectations, the analyst should attempt to identify the weaknesses in the data he uses in his forecast. Estimates of possible errors in future sales, value added, and the labor productivity forecasts are the most important in this examination.[4]

Table 6-5 shows how a range estimate is constructed for the Midwest Company. In this illustration, different value-added ratios to the $27,600,000 sales forecast are related to different labor productivity levels that result from different labor productivity rates. Similar matrices can be constructed for different sales forecasts.

These estimates indicate that for sales of $27,600,000, manpower requirements range from 905 employees to 1,115 under the various postulations. It was felt that the labor productivity estimate error would most probably be on the high side. A

TABLE 6-5

MIDWEST COMPANY RANGE ESTIMATES OF MANPOWER
NEEDS
(Sales Forecast: $27,600,000)

Labor Productivity Rate (Per Cent)	Labor Productivity Level (Per Employee)	Value Added as a Percentage of Sales Revenue		
		48% ($13.25mm.)	50% ($13.80mm.)	52% ($14.35mm.)
5	$12,895	1,027	1,070	1,115
7	14,044	945	985	1,020
8	14,639	905	945	980

---

[4] A tendency exists for potential forecast errors to behave in a self-correcting manner. If sales are overestimated, it is possible that capital investment will be less rapid than planned because of lower than anticipated amounts of cash, profits, and demand for capacity. This will tend to reduce labor productivity gains and to increase manpower needs. Thus the labor force will move toward the original estimate despite the lower sales.

second best point estimate for manpower was therefore set at 1,070 employees. The the third best point estimate involved the eight per cent productivity rate and was set at 945 employees. The working range interval around the 985 employment forecasts is thus established at a minimum of 945 and a maximum of 1,070. Examination of the impact of various assumptions regarding labor productivity and value added on manpower levels may be facilitated by the construction of graphs which plot the relationship between the three variables of labor productivity, value added, and manpower.

FORECASTING PAYROLL GROUPS

The total manpower forecast can be divided into major payroll groups to estimate probable future managerial manpower requirements. An analysis of the past composition of the workforce aids in the development of an estimate of its probable future composition. Table 6-6 shows the former composition of the Midwest Company.

Salaried employment as a percentage of the workforce was cut in the last two years because of hiring restrictions. These restrictions were part of a cost reduction program designed to improve the company's profit position.

Discussions with company officials, held to estimate foresee-

TABLE 6-6

MIDWEST COMPANY WORKFORCE COMPOSITION

Year	Hourly Employees (Per Cent)	Salaried Non-exempt Employees (Per Cent)	Salaried-exempt Employees (Per Cent)
1	76	17	7
2	75	18	7
3	72	20	8
4	68	19	13
5	64	20	16
6	63	22	15
7	59	24	17
8	57	23	20
9	59	20	21
10	64	18	18

able developments in the workforce, indicated that the current salaried workforce was at minimum staffing and that additional hiring would be needed in the near future. At the same time, an objective of holding the salaried non-exempt group to its same relative percentage seemed desirable as a cost control device. The exempt group employment estimate was set at 20 per cent of the workforce to allow for growth in management and engineering. The resulting hourly portion of the employment total is therefore 62 per cent, as shown in 6-7.[5]

TABLE 6-7

MIDWEST COMPANY EMPLOYMENT GROUP MANPOWER
FORECASTS

	Current Year (Per Cent)	Number	Forecast Year (Per Cent)	Number
Total employment	100	897	100	985
Hourly employment	64	572	62	611
Salaried non-exempt	18	159	18	177
Salaried-exempt	18	166	20	197

A MAJOR FORECASTING PROBLEM

Several problems associated with the labor-productivity forecast method have been suggested. These include data availability, measurement of output and input, and the reliability of forecast information. A major problem not yet examined now requires special attention.

This involves determining whether the current manpower staffing reflects good manpower utilization with respect to the output being produced. For example, a company may be currently overstaffed with salaried personnel. Future growth in

[5] This approach to estimating the composition of the workforce is obviously a gross approach that lacks sophistication. It is possible to develop productivity rates and levels for each employment group, to forecast manpower for each group, and then to add the totals. Correlation analysis might also be explored to examine the relationships between employment groups. An important question that needs attention is the influence of the salaried-exempt personnel on the productivity of hourly personnel. As the manpower forecasting effort matures, further analytical work in this area should be undertaken.

output in this situation can be realized without a normal increase in manpower because of the excess salaried manpower capacity. This would result in higher than normal future labor productivity gains. The opposite situation can also exist where the organization may be short of manpower in certain activities. As it catches up to its needs, the labor productivity growth is likely to be less than would normally be expected.

Adequacy of staffing also affects the historic productivity data. Organizations may operate for several years with excessive salaried manpower, an indication of lower labor productivity than could have been achieved. In the Midwest Company, for example, personnel department managers said the company did not attempt to control hiring of clerical personnel to any great extent during years three through seven and was probably overstaffed with female non-exempt employees during this period.

One approach to the problem is through ratio analysis. Here staffing of one employment group is compared with total employment or some other figure. When the ratio deviates significantly from trend figures, it may indicate that manpower is above or below the "ideal" level. This might be true providing unusual conditions did not dictate changes in the ratio. In the Midwest Company, for example, the salaried non-exempt workforce rose to between 20 and 24 per cent of the total workforce during years five through eight. This ratio, compared with a level below 20 per cent in all the other years, suggests possible overstaffing during those years. It is not likely that the hourly workforce was understaffed in years five through eight because its level is closely related to the actual physical production of goods.

The ratio of employment in various departments to total employment might also be examined to identify over- or understaffing conditions. For example, the ratio of personnel department employment to total employment may normally decline as total employment rises. If the ratio of personnel department employment to total employment rose when it was expected to fall, examination of the reasons would be in order. The same technique is used to evaluate staffing in other departments. The engineering group might be evaluated against total employment, new projects, or project dollar value. Production overhead manpower might be evaluated against total production employment or output.

What are suggested here are types of productivity studies for various employment groups and organizational units. Changes in ratios will occur as company operations change. Significant ratio deviations from normal trend patterns then might become the subjects of investigation.

It may well be that for companies that attempt to maintain control over their manpower levels, salaried employment will normalize around an "ideal" staffing level over time. In these companies over- or understaffing conditions are recognized through control techniques and corrective adjustments are made.

Another method of determining the adequacy of employment staffing is from the subjective evaluations of persons involved in manpower management. The employment manager should have opinions regarding the staffing adequacy through his experience with manpower requisitions, layoffs, and separations. Other men concerned with internal efficiency — such as industrial engineers, systems specialists, and organization planners — also have opinions that might be less biased than those of department managers. The attitudes of top management and of the controller towards cost reduction at various points in time also influence the evaluation of past manpower staffing levels.

Evaluation of the relationship of past and present actual manpower levels to the "ideal" level is not easy. Primary attention should be given to the salaried employment group because it responds less quickly to changes in output levels. To overcome the lack of established principles and theories in this area of manpower planning requires added resourcefulness on the part of the manpower planner.[6]

---

[6] An approach to the problem is a statistical analysis of current manpower staffing suggested by Albert Drui. Regression equations developed from a study of input-output relationships are used to evaluate current manpower levels. Differences between actual manpower and the manpower developed from the equations are investigated for possible action. This approach requires an identification of significant and accurately measurable output units for the activity being evaluated. See Albert B. Drui, "The Use of Regression Equations to Predict Manpower Requirements," *Management Science,* July 1963, pp. 669-677.

CONCLUSION

The labor productivity approach to manpower forecasting is more meaningful and realistic than manpower forecasts based on a method that is not related to future output. The technique is not without its problems, but adequate methods are available to handle most of them.

It is probable that new manpower forecasting techniques will be developed as more companies seek information on their future manpower needs. Refinements will be made in labor productivity analysis. The measurement of capital productivity and its impact on labor requirements will be clarified. As companies increase their interest in labor productivity measurement, more attention will be given to capital productivity studies.

The accuracy of a manpower forecast (i.e., as forecast versus actual employment) will vary with the reliability of the data and the ability of the forecaster to anticipate changing economic conditions. Because the business firm operates in a dynamic environment, the forecast should be updated annually to reflect changes in the economic structure. Each effort should improve the forecaster's ability to estimate future requirements. The first effort requires the greatest amount of historical work; subsequent efforts can probe more deeply into variables not previously considered. This additional probing should improve the quality of the forecast.

As indicated earlier, organizations that have an economics or statistical research group may rely on these experts to make manpower forecasts. Economic models and operations research techniques may be used by these groups. If someone else makes the manpower forecast, the manpower planner should have an understanding of the forecast methods employed. This understanding enables him to interpret and use the forecast more intelligently.

CHAPTER 7

THE MANPOWER FORECAST AND CORPORATE PROFIT OBJECTIVES

Financial management is not the province of the manpower planner, but the effectiveness of the manpower manager rests in part on his ability to understand the relationship of key financial variables to manpower management.

Future manpower requirements depend in part on the financial resources of the organization. Manpower, in turn, influences finances because of its associated payroll cost. An understanding of how the manpower forecast relates to certain financial variables projected in other forecasts is therefore important in manpower planning.

In this chapter the relationship between the manpower forecast and the profit plan will be examined. The discussion covers material manpower managers do not normally explore. Financial management is not the province of the manpower planner, but the effectiveness of the manpower manager rests in part on his ability to understand the relationship of key financial variables to manpower management.

Essentially, the idea to be developed is that the manpower requirements indicated by the forecast have an associated wage cost. This cost affects profit potential, and thus the return on investment and the return on the sales dollar. Increases in labor productivity lower the wages that would otherwise be paid and thus positively affect profits. Labor productivity gains, however, most often result from added use of capital in the form of plant and equipment. When a company raises its investment base to improve labor productivity, its return on investment is affected. When these relationships are considered in the manpower program, the planner is able to discuss his forecasts in terms of profit objectives, investment levels, and productivity rates.

163

IDENTIFYING PROFIT OBJECTIVES

Much of the literature on corporate profit management centers on the nature of profit objectives, on the concept of a satisfactory versus an optimal profit level, or on short- versus long-range profit objectives. The use of target market shares and their effect on profits in planning are also discussed.

After examining the general economic procedures of many companies in relation to their profit objectives, Neil Chamberlain makes this statement of corporate profit objectives:

> ...we find that most firms which budget have objectives toward which the budget, as an operating plan, is directed. In most firms this objective is a rate of profit (or rate range) which arises out of experience or comparisons or expectations. It is this more or less designed profit goal, rather than some hypothetical maximum profit, which informs business planning. The profit rate may be computed against sales, or with increasing frequency, investment. In the latter case, investment may be construed as total assets (gross or net of depreciation) or as net worth.[1]

The present analysis of manpower in relationship to profit objectives is through the use of a model. The values assigned to given variables in the model influence the values that should exist in other variables. The following four points describe the key elements in this analysis:

1. Profits as a percentage of sales revenue and as a per cent return on investment are meaningful long-range profit objectives. A forecast of value added is related to these kinds of profit goals.

2. The relationship of estimated future labor productivity and value added governs future total employment and wage estimates. These estimates should be compatible with the profit forecast.

3. The growth rate of labor productivity (value added per employee) is related to the rate by which the company adds fixed capital to its operations. The probable amount of fixed capital needed to achieve a labor productivity level can be estimated by examining the projected labor productivity rate.

4. The fixed capital required to achieve a labor productivity growth rate becomes part of the investment base against which profits are measured. This asset formation must, therefore,

---

[1] Neil Chamberlain, *The Firm* (New York: McGraw-Hill Book Company, 1962), p. 65.

satisfy both labor productivity objectives and profit objectives.

These statements indicate that the model consists of a series of interrelated variables that must be satisfied simultaneously. Through its use the planner is able to determine whether the manpower forecast is realistic in light of other economic forecasts. The set of numbers used to illustrate the relationships presented in the model was selected for ease in manipulation (and thus sometimes is rounded in the text). The numbers are not intended to demonstrate either good or poor financial management principles.

TABLE 7-1
SUMMARY OF DATA USED IN EXAMPLE

Item	Year n	Year n + 10
1. Sales Revenue	$50,000,000	$100,000,000
2. Earnings per Sales Dollar	12%	10%
3. Pre-tax Earnings	$ 6,000,000	$ 10,000,000
4. Earnings on Investment	15%	18%
5. Investment	$40,000,000	$ 55,556,000
6. Current Assets	$20,000,000	$ 27,778,000
7. Fixed Assets	$20,000,000	$ 27,778,000
8. Value Added per Sales Dollar	46%	42%
9. Value Added (Basic Output)	$23,200,000	$ 42,000,000
10. Value Added per Wage Dollar	$1.45	$1.45
11. Total Wages	$16,000,000	$ 28,965,000
12. Wages per Employee	$ 8,000	$ 10,752
13. Total Employment	2,000	2,694
14. Value Added per Employee	$ 11,600	$ 15,590
15. Annual Labor Productivity Rate	3.0%	3.0%

FEASIBILITY ANALYSIS —
GIVEN FIXED ASSET GROWTH RATE TO LABOR
PRODUCTIVITY GROWTH RATE OF 1.5 TO 1.0

Planned Levels vs. Needed	Planned	Needed	Deficiency
16. Fixed Assets	$27,778,000	$31,060,000	$ 3,282,000
17. Current Assets	$27,778,000	$27,778,000	
18. Total Assets	$55,556,000	$58,838,000	$ 3,282,000
19. Return on Investment	18%	18%	
20. Earnings Based on Target Return	$10,000,000	$10,600,000	$ 600,000

FIGURE 7-1

EARNINGS AND SALES

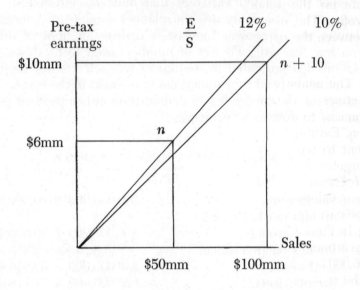

FIGURE 7-2

EARNINGS AND INVESTMENT

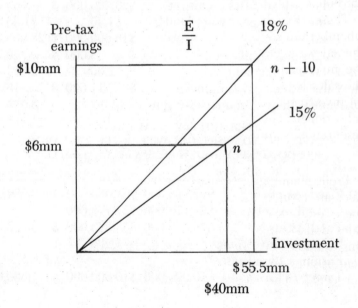

Table 7-1 includes the current year values, and the values for forecast year ten with a three per cent labor productivity rate for the period. Also shown are estimates of sales and profits. The discussion does not explore the growth pattern between the current year and the forecast year.

PROFIT PLANNING GOALS

The analysis begins with an examination of the profit objectives of the company. In the illustration, sales revenue is forecast to double and reach $100,000,000 by the end of year ten. Earnings per sales dollar are expected to fall from 12 per cent to ten per cent. With sales of $100,000,000 and profits targeted at ten per cent of sales revenue, future total pre-tax profits are estimated at $10,000,000. (See Figure 7-1. Current year values are designated by the letter "n" and the ten-year forecast figures by "$n + 10$.")

In Figure 7-2, the relationship between pre-tax earnings and investment is shown. Current investment is $40,000,000, profits $6,000,000, and the pre-tax return on investment 15 per cent. The ten-year profit plan calls for a targeted pre-tax return on investment of 18 per cent. The forecast of $10,000,000 in profits from sales revenue means that investment must be around the $55,500,000 level for the 18 per cent return to be realized.

These two diagrams link the twin profit objectives that Chamberlain suggests govern many profit plans. Working from the sales forecast to the return on investment suggests that the investment level is perhaps more easily controlled than the sales level. This does not mean that the concept of return on investment is less important than the concept of return on sales dollar. The opposite is true from the economic view of resource allocation.

MANPOWER AND THE PROFIT PLAN

Profit planning of this nature means that the future costs of sales are estimated to determine profits per sales dollar. From these estimates the expected "value-added" portion of the sales dollar can be determined. Figure 7-3 indicates that in this example, value added is currently $23,200,000 or 46.4 per cent of sales revenue. The estimate of future value added is 42 per cent. (This decline might result from expected higher

FIGURE 7-3

VALUE ADDED AND SALES

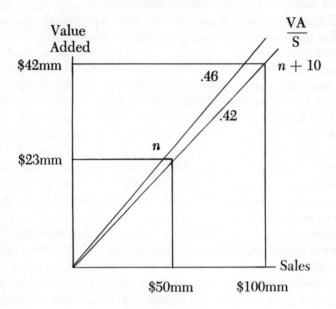

FIGURE 7-4

VALUE ADDED AND WAGES

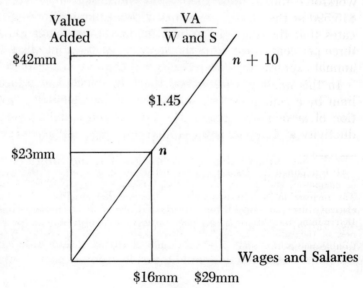

prices for materials and changes in the make-versus-buy mix.) The 42 per cent level means that the future value added on forecast sales of $100,000,000 is $42,000,000.

In Figure 7-4 the relationship of wages and salaries to value added is shown. The current wage bill is $16,000,000, or $1.00 of wages for every $1.45 of value added. It is assumed that the minimum labor productivity objective of the company is to keep this ratio from falling, even though average wages are expected to rise by three per cent.[2] Against a projected value added of $42,000,000, the ratio indicates that total wages of slightly under $29,000,000 can be tolerated and still be consistent with the profit plan.

In Figure 7-5, the relationship between wages and total employment, the current employment level is 2,000 workers at an average expense of $8,000 per employee. With a three per cent average annual increase in expenses per employee, the average employee wage at the end of ten years will be $10,750. If a total wage bill of nearly $29,000,000 is allowable under the profit plan, a total workforce of 2,694 is permissible.

The relationship of the workforce level to value added is shown in Figure 7-6. The current value added is $23,200,000, current employment 2,000, and value added per employee $11,600. A projected value added of $42,000,000 and an upper workforce tolerance of 2,694 make value added per employee $15,590 at the end of ten years. (This productivity level indicates that the average productivity rate during the period is three per cent — just equal to the three per cent increase in the annual expense per employee.)

In this analysis total wages are kept within an acceptable limit by a ceiling on total employment. This ceiling is a function of labor productivity. The assumption to hold labor productivity at $1.45 of value added per wage dollar means that

---

[2] It is important to evaluate this productivity ratio. If it reflects poor utilization of manpower, and thus of labor dollars, attempts should be made to raise it. Any increase in labor productivity is desirable, providing a decline in total efficiency does not result from less effective use of other production factors. Determining the correctness of current manpower levels, and thus the correctness of the value added to labor dollar expense ratio, is difficult. Especially troublesome is the estimate of the proper staffing for indirect hourly workers and salaried employees.

FIGURE 7-5

EMPLOYMENT AND WAGES

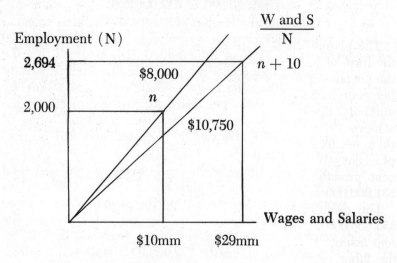

FIGURE 7-6

EMPLOYMENT AND VALUE
ADDED

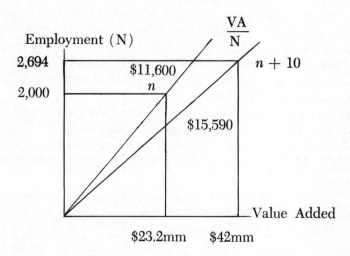

all wage increases to individuals are matched by productivity increases.

FIXED ASSETS AND PRODUCTIVITY

The planner's attention now turns to the stock of capital in the form of fixed assets and its relationship to manpower. For the purpose of exposition, it will be assumed that for each one per cent increase in the net stock of fixed assets, labor productivity increases by about two-thirds of a per cent. To achieve a three per cent annual increase in labor productivity, then, net fixed assets must be formed at an annual rate of 4.5 per cent.[3] If net fixed assets are now $20,000,000, a 4.5 per cent growth rate means they should increase to just over $31,000,000 at the end of ten years.[4]

The profit plan, however, calls for a total investment of $55,500,000 in ten years split equally between fixed and current assets.[5] If $31,000,000 in fixed assets is required to sustain the labor productivity growth, only $24,500,000 of the total investment is available for current asset usage. This sum appears inadequate because $20,000,000 in current assets is currently required for sales of $50,000,000 and the forecast projects sales to be $100,000,000. If total assets were increased to raise fixed assets to $31,000,000, profits would have to increase by $600,000 to enable the company to earn its targeted 18 per cent return on investment. (These figures are shown in the Feasibility Analysis of Table 7-1.) This feasibility analysis of labor productivity and manpower requirements suggests that the manpower aspects of the profit plan are not feasible because the fixed asset level required to sustain the labor productivity growth is not provided in the profit plan. Further

---

[3] It is assumed that the company is operating at, or near, capacity. Significant labor productivity gains are therefore not possible through increased utilization of existing facilities.

[4] Actual additions to facilities will exceed the net increase. If a five per cent annual depreciation rate is applied to plant and equipment, and net facilities are added in a straight-line manner in this illustration, the total outlay for new facilities (in dollar terms) is about $23,000,000.

[5] Weston suggests that the ratio of net fixed assets to total assets is in the 30 to 50 per cent range for manufacturing firms, with higher ratios in producer equipment and materials firms, and lower ratios in consumer goods firms. See J. Fred Weston, *Managerial Finance* (2nd. Ed.) (New York: Holt, Rinehart, and Winston, 1966), p. 134.

examinations of the relationships presented in this example
is therefore necessary.

THE TARGET LABOR PRODUCTIVITY APPROACH

The illustration above began with profit-planning objectives
and examined labor requirements with respect to them. The
planner can begin by setting a target labor productivity rate
that exceeds expected average employee wage increases and
then observe its impact on other variables.

To illustrate, assume that a five per cent labor productivity
increase is desirable in order to more than match an expected
three per cent annual average wage increase. The five per cent
productivity rate is possible if assets are formed at a 7.5 per
cent rate using the previous estimate of the relationship of
these two rates. Value added per employee will be $18,900
after ten years if labor productivity increases five per cent
annually. The profit plan calls for a value added of $42,000,000.
This means that about 2,220 workers will be needed to produce
this value added. If average wages rise three per cent annually,
the cost per employee is $10,750 and the total wage bill will
be just under $23,900,000. (Under the three per cent produc-
tivity analysis, total wages were set at just under $29,000,000.)

This lower labor cost from increased productivity should
raise profits. For simplicity, assume profits will be expected to
rise by $4,000,000. (All the labor savings would not go into
profits because of the added depreciation, maintenance, and
other expenses associated with higher fixed asset usage.) If
$4,000,000 more in profits were realized, the return on invest-
ment would rise to 25 per cent, if total investment did not
increase beyond $55,500,000.

To achieve this five per cent labor productivity rate, however, fixed assets would have to increase to over $41,000,000
versus the $31,000,000 level in the three per cent analysis. If
this $10,000,000 difference is added to the investment base to
increase it to $65,500,000, the return on investment under the
five per cent target labor productivity rate would be approximately 21.3 per cent. This would be a significant improvement over the objective of an 18 per cent return on investment.

The results of this analysis suggest that the profit plan and
the manpower forecast should be closely linked. It is perhaps

naive to think that the mere addition of new plant and equipment will generate higher labor productivity, yet examination
of historical trends usually shows much more than a merely
casual relationship between the two rates.

In this example, a 470-man reduction in forecast manpower
is achieved with the five per cent productivity rate compared
with the three per cent rate. The annual labor saving in year
ten is over $5,000,000 if average wages are $10,750 per person.
Additional savings would be realized in the other years of the
forecast period.

If an analysis of profit and manpower forecasts yields a
situation like that presented above, a rather thorough economic
analysis is required. The planner needs to determine whether
the higher productivity rate is feasible in terms of potential
new uses of fixed capital and of funds available for investment
purposes. Even where the analysis indicates that both these
conditions can be met, and that investment to raise labor productivity is profitable in light of the cost of capital and alternative uses of it, the profit plan may need revision because of
considerations of savings in manpower expense.

LABOR EXPENSE AND THE PROFIT PLAN

Another possible method of analysis focuses on the projected
labor expense portion of the profit plan. The projected total
wage bill divided by the projected average wage per employee yields a manpower estimate. A number of long-range
financial plans rest on this approach, although the resulting
manpower figures may be incompatible with previous labor
productivity rates and with the probable rate during the forecast period.

In the example, this type of analysis might begin with a target wage bill of $24,600,000. With projected labor costs of
$10,750 per employee, a labor force estimate of 2,288 is de-
veloped. This manpower level will require an annual labor
productivity rate of nearly five per cent. Unless the long-range
budget includes major capital expansion, however, either the
wage bill will exceed $24,600,000 or the forecast of 2,288
employees will be too low. This is asssuming as previously
that the capital formation rate is in a three-to-two relationship

with the labor productivity rate and that wages per employee rise to the $10,750 level.

CONCLUSION

It has been seen that the analysis of the manpower planning relationship to profit planning may begin with any of several elements of the overall planned model. Further, the relationships among economic variables can assume many forms. The values assigned to labor productivity, return on investment, and value added determine the solutions developed. The model can be made more complex by introducing different labor productivity rates and different wage increase rates for managerial, clerical, and hourly employees. The capital structure examination can be expanded to include analysis of current assets, working capital, and depreciation.

Computer simulation of the model can be used to study the effects on the variables under different hypotheses. Simulations permit examination of a wide variety of situations with relative ease and help manpower planners to see the relationships of manpower to economic objectives more clearly.

It is important for the manpower planner to recognize the relationship between manpower requirements and economic objectives. This does not mean that he engages in economic or financial planning; his analysis will show, however, the ways in which the manpower aspects of company plans relate to profit and capital formation aspects.

When briefing top management on long-range manpower requirements, the planner should be capable of discussing the effects of his forecasts on profits and investment. Unless he is able to do this, he may not obtain the support he needs for his activity. In addition, when the manpower planner relates his efforts to economic variables, other planners may become more concerned with the manpower factors implicit in their work. This should result in improved total resource planning for the company.

CHAPTER 7 APPENDIX

THE RETURN ON INVESTMENT CONCEPT

The return on investment concept is a widely used means of measuring economic performance.[1] Its exact meaning, however, is often unclear. Because of the difficulty in evaluating assets accurately, distortion may arise in the use of the concept even when the nature of "investment" is clearly understood.

For manpower planning purposes, "total assets" used in the production process appear to be the most meaningful definition of investments. Manpower levels are influenced by all the resources used in the production process. Thus, assets financed by debt capital are as important to manpower utilization as assets financed by equity capital. The valuation of total assets, however, is not an easy task, and analysts differ as to the proper method to use in the valuation exercise.

Most commonly, the book value of the assets (net of de-

---

[1] Chamberlain, *op. cit.*, pp. 57-65. The formula used by many companies to measure return on investment is:

$$\frac{\text{profits}}{\text{sales}} \quad x \quad \frac{\text{sales}}{\text{investment}} = \text{return on investment}$$

This formulation was pioneered by the duPont Company in the 1920's and is regarded as a basic and traditional approach to financial planning. In the duPont methodology, investment is the composite of working capital (inventories, receivables, and cash) and gross permanent investment. Profits are determined by sales minus the cost of sales (production, selling, delivery, and administrative expenses). See "How the duPont Organization Appraises Its Performance," by T. C. Davis, *American Management Association*, Financial Management Series, No. 94 (New York: American Management Association, 1950). The simplified measure of return on investment is profits divided by investment.

175

preciation) is used for valuation purposes.[2] This practice results in the current assets being valued in current dollar terms and the bulk of the fixed assets being valued in historic dollar terms. It may also mean that fully depreciated assets still being used are not reflected in the asset base.[3] Such problems as these have led to an increased emphasis on current dollar valuation of assets (e.g., the security market valuation of outstanding obligations of the firm). The merit of currrent dollar valuation in long-range financial planning is that it focuses attention on earning a return on the current value of the assets, not on their historic value.[4] Placing an accurate current value on assets is difficult, however. In using the security market valuation approach, for example, market fluctuations which have little relationship to economic value may enter the calculations.

An awareness of these issues helps the manpower planner to fully understand his work. His efforts will be guided by the conventions used by financial analysts and accountants. Historic book value is the common approach to asset valuation. Long-range profit planning relationships to manpower planning will therefore frequently depend on this valuation method. If replacement cost or some other means is used to value assets for planning and evaluation, the manpower planner may have to follow that procedure in his studies because of the availability of data.

---

[2] *Op. cit.*, pp. 58-65. Chamberlain says that total assets is the most common definition of investment for the return on investment analysis. The valuation of assets takes many different forms, according to Chamberlain, ranging from original book value to replacement value. He argues that net worth (stockholders' equity) is a better economic basis for measuring the rate of return. This focuses attention on the return to the owners of the firm and permits leverage effects of non-owner debt capital to be reflected in the profits of the stockholders. See also, James H. Miller, "A Glimpse at Practice in Calculating and Using Return on Investment," *N.A.A. Bulletin,* June 1960, pp. 65-76. Miller surveyed leading American companies regarding their practices in measuring return on investment. His results suggest that different investment bases may be used to measure internal profit performance and performance against competitors and other leading firms.

[3] Many other problems of this general nature are associated with the rate of return concept. See William J. Vatter, "Does the Rate of Return Measure Business Efficiency?" *N.A.A. Bulletin,* January 1959, pp. 38-48.

[4] The 1962 annual report of the Sheraton Corporation of America contains an officers' estimate of the current value of fixed assets which is 50 per cent larger than the book value figure.

THE CAPITAL TURNOVER CONCEPT

The concept of capital turnover (sales revenue divided by the level of investment) is related to the concept of return on investment and profits as a percentage of sales revenue. This is a profit-planning tool companies use to help disclose the effectiveness of capital resources in generating revenue. Measurement by profits per sales dollar helps to highlight the cost side of return on investment. Capital turnover highlights the resource utilization side and shows how return on investment is influenced by the effectiveness with which the company uses its resources. Capital turnover in the chapter illustration in the current year is 1.25 — based on sales of $50,000,000 and an investment of $40,000,000. In year "$n$ plus 10" the turnover is 1.80 on sales of $100,000,000 and investment of $55,500,000. This large increase in capital turnover is implicit in the example because of the projected decline in the ratio of profits to sales.

CHAPTER 8

CONTROL AND EVALUATION

*Perfect balance in a business exists only on the organization chart.
A living business is always in a state of imbalance, growing here and
shrinking there, overdoing one thing and neglecting another.*
— PETER DRUCKER

Accompanying the design of manpower plans should be
control procedures which enable the planner to evaluate his
efforts. These procedures will assume a variety of forms, depending on the activity being evaluated. The objective of
control systems is to improve performance. The planner determines how actual performance compares with desired performance and takes action to make the two conditions equal.
The data generated in this activity also serve in the design of
new programs and may cause abandonment of unworkable
plans.

The literature on the subject of control is growing rapidly.
New techniques for improving the control of various organizational activities are developed as management strives to
improve its performance. Computers enable the planner to
process and evaluate vast amounts of data for control purposes.
It is possible now to talk about "real time" control systems,
which theoretically means being able to take immediate corrective action when deviations from planned performance arise.

ESTABLISHING PERFORMANCE STANDARDS

The first ingredients in the control process are the goals and
standards established to be used in measuring performance.
These performance criteria should relate to the overall objectives in the plan. If care is not taken, standards may be
established which relate only to a subordinate objective of
the plan. If this happens performance may be measured in a

limited fashion and the erroneous conclusion drawn that every-
thing is satisfactory.

Take, for example, a plan involving the acceleration of the
development of younger managers. If performance is measured
only by upward mobility patterns, planned objectives may
appear to be met. But the accelerated development program exists to provide a sufficient number of qualified men for
higher level vacancies. Unless the qualifications of these men
to assume added responsibilities are also measured the overall
objective of the plan may fail to be met.

In long-range planning efforts it is also important to establish
shorter-run objectives to serve as milestones on the path to
the more distant goals. These milestones enable the planner to
evaluate performance through time and to take corrective
action before the long-range plan is seriously threatened with
failure.

Both quantitative and qualitative standards are required in
most manpower planning activities. The quantitative criteria
are usually easier to establish than the qualitative. Numbers
tend to provide a certain amount of objectivity an are relatively easy to determine for the various quantitati objectives.

In the qualitative area the planner frequently lacks numerical methods of measuring performance. How, for example, does
he determine numerically whether an early retirement program is performing satisfactorily? Or how does he evaluate
numerically the quality of the design of a future organization
structure? Sometimes the measuring problem rises from a lack
of experience in a planning activity. But lack of convenient
measuring devices does not provide an escape from the necessity to evaluate.

If he lacks clear objective yardsticks, he can still use subjective estimates of performance. He can enumerate the elements of a plan and weight them with respect to importance.
Later, when he observes actual performance, he can estimate
the amount of success of each activity in percentage terms.
This kind of evaluation may eventually furnish insights for
setting more objective performance criteria as substitutes for
the initial highly subjective criteria.

Another approach is to identify sub-objectives of the overall

FIGURE 8-1

POSSIBLE GOALS AND STANDARDS FOR CONTROL PURPOSES

Activity	Goals and Standards
Recruitment	Annual college manpower quotas based on forecasts.
Selection	Hire college graduates from top half of class.
Placement	Assign highest rated managers to most critical jobs.
Managerial appraisal	Identification of strongest and weakest managers based on quintile rankings of personnel.
Development	Target improvement in performance appraisal results for below average managers.
Mobility patterns	Reduction in early development of new managers by one-fourth current time requirements.
Retirements	Planned pattern for volume of annual retirements by levels and units.
Information system	Up-to-date information of total manpower and individual managers easily available.
Compensation	Maintain total wage bill within forecast limits.
Organization planning	Identify potential new positions and manpower capable of filling them.
Research projects	Obtain tangible economic benefits from one-third of manpower research projects.

plan that can be measured numerically. Frequently these will be shorter-run objectives that are compatible with the long-range plan. The management development program may have an objective of broadening the experience base of men for eventual top management positions. Success of the short-run plan perhaps can be numerically measured through reductions in the number of vacant positions, the new hires of outside personnel, or the transfers in from other organizational units.

Figure 8-1 contains a list of manpower planning activities and examples of goals or standards that might be associated with them. For control purposes, several standards would exist for each activity, some short-run and others long-run in nature.

THE MONITOR STAGE

The monitor stage in control involves the sampling and measurement of performance. In a temperature control system, a thermostat continuously samples and measures the heat level. In a manpower control system the planner takes samples less frequently and relies on written reports and tables to measure performance. The monitor system should record accurately and unambiguously. It should also provide information which helps to explain the factors leading to the performance quality. The frequency with which performance is monitored relates to the timing of desired corrective action. In some activities, below-standard performance can be tolerated for a longer time period than in other activities, or it may take longer to devise the corrective action program for some activities than for others. These factors govern the timing of the monitor system. (Figure 8-2 is a diagram of the control process.)

THE EVALUATION STATE

Two considerations govern the evaluation of data the planner receives from the monitoring system. One is to determine if corrective action is required because of the current level of performance. To make this decision he must first ascertain if the current performance deviates from pre-established standards and whether the deviations are within tolerable limits.

The change in performance must also be evaluated. This is called the change in the closure rate of performance to standard. The planner may, for example, find performance is outside acceptable limits but is improving at a rate of change which will soon make it acceptable. In such a situation, no corrective action may be necessary because adequate corrective forces

FIGURE 8-2

THE CONTROL PROCESS

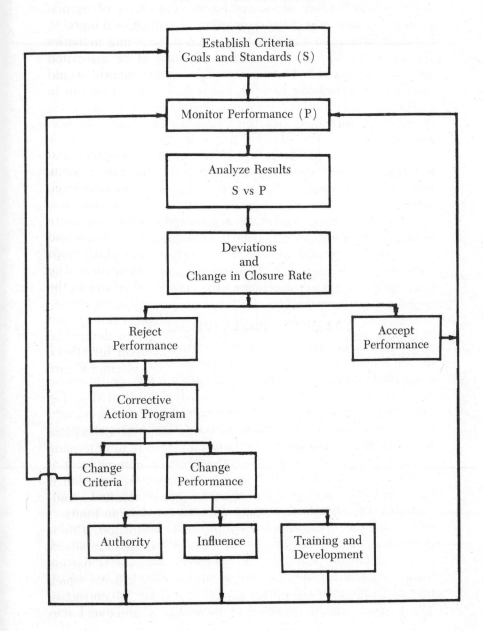

are already at work. Or he may find that performance is currently satisfactory in terms of deviation, but will soon become unacceptable because of various forces at work. For example, an attrition rate among managers may be currently acceptable but deteriorating at a rate that will soon make it unacceptable. By observing the period-to-period changes in the attrition rate he may be able to take corrective action before an unsatisfactory performance level is reached.

The interrelationships between deviations of actual from standard performance and the dynamics of change in performance enable the planner to decide whether to accept current activity or to take action. If he accepts the performance, he recycles and takes new observations with the monitor system. If performance is unacceptable, he takes corrective action.

If he has established several criteria standards for an activity he may determine performance is unacceptable in a few respects, but acceptable in most of the others, and partial corrective action is necessary. The planner must avoid correcting one aspect of such performance at the expense of other aspects which are more important.

TAKING CORRECTIVE ACTION

Corrective action can take two forms. The planner may decide that the reasons current performance is not acceptable are sufficiently good to cause changes in the performance standard. A manpower hiring restraint that originated in the manpower forecast is perhaps being exceeded. If this is because output levels are higher than forecast, the staffing criteria probably require an upward revision.

The second form of corrective action is to change actual performance to make it conform to the standards. Both organizational authority and personal influence can be utilized to accomplish this. Directives supported by the sanction and reward system of the organization exemplify the use of authority; persuasion, communications skills, and motivational devices of an individual are examples of influence. The cooperation a manpower planner obtains from using his influence is directly related to his own reputation and status in the organization. The planner who is regarded as having good judgment and thorough knowledge of manpower issues will gain greater cooperation than one who lacks this reputation. Well-conceived manpower forecasts that relate to profit plans, and a thorough analysis of managerial manpower needs by organizational levels, are two ways a manpower planner can gain status.

In manpower situations power in the form either of authority or influence is frequently inadequate to achieve desired performance levels. If the personnel involved in a program lack the ability and skill required to perform satisfactorily, training and development work are required. For this reason, the manpower planner must carefully interpret the reasons for unsatisfactory performance. Problems of obtaining satisfactory data on managerial performance and potential, for example, will not improve if managers lack guidance and skill in making evaluations of their subordinates.

After corrective action is taken, the planner awaits the next monitor report on the program status. In some activities the report may be made a year later; in others, at the end of the next month. Throughout the entire control cycle, he should be evaluating the adequacy of his control procedures. Does the monitor provide the right data? Is he able to evaluate the data intelligently? Do corrective actions achieve the desired results? Such questions should be examined regularly to improve the control system, performance, and plans.

CONTROL DEVICES

The methods the planner uses to monitor and evaluate performance should be tailored to the activity under control. An annual report of overall manpower planning activities which summarizes that year's performance against objectives is perhaps the minimum requirement. Current status reports on selective activities are needed more frequently when corrective action is required to correct below-standard performance.

Charts and graphs are useful in manpower control. Figure 8-3 is an example of a manpower staffing control form used to display the relationship of manpower in one category against that of another. In this illustration, engineering manpower is plotted against salaried-exempt manpower, to help the planner understand and control engineering staffing and costs. Similar charts can be used for manpower groups which are not directly

FIGURE 8-3

RELATIONSHIP OF ENGINEERING MANPOWER TO TOTAL
SALARIED-EXEMPT MANPOWER

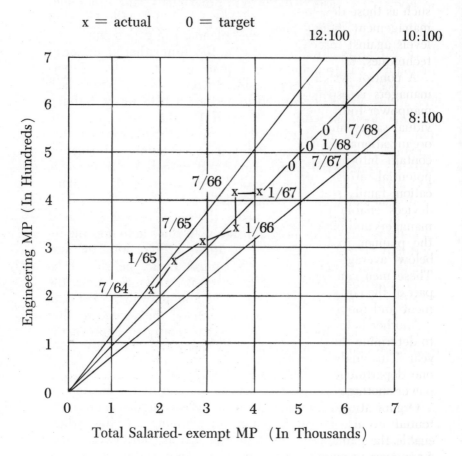

ENGINEERING MANPOWER BUDGET PERFORMANCE
(In Thousands)

Date	7/64	1/65	7/65	1/66	7/66	1/67	7/67	1/68	7/68
Budget	1,100	1,500	1,800	2,100	2,400	2,600	2,800	3,100	3,300
Actual	1,200	1,680	1,800	1,980	2,460	2,500	—	—	—
Deviation + or −	+100	+180	0	−120	+60	−100	—	—	—

tied to current production levels and are thus somewhat difficult to control.

Analysis of managerial manpower through the use of tables such as those developed in Chapter 4 is a means of evaluating management staffing plans. The tracking of actual manpower levels against forecast levels provides insight into forecasting techniques.

A control system for the career performance of individual managers is especially important in manpower planning. A manpower form (or computer program) which plots the individual salary and performance progress of a manager against organizational norms is easily constructed. The form can also contain information on past assignments, performance and potential ratings, and demographic information such as education, family status, language skills, and job interests. These devices enable the planner to monitor the performance of managers and plan for their future utilization. They also enable the planner to identify men who are performing above or below average for longer periods than the current year. These men can be given special attention by the planner as part of the corrective action program in management development and mobility.

Another helpful control procedure in career management is to determine the progress of promotable manpower during the year. This analysis may reveal that while promotable men in one department are not advancing, a department with manpower shortages is promoting managers with lower ratings.

Organization charts color coded to indicate promotion potential are also useful in qualitative manpower control. They enable the planner quickly to visualize the relative quality of manpower in various organizational units and the number of back-up men with promotion potential for each higher level position. Comparison of these charts over time informs the planner about the progress of the organization in preparing for future needs. Finally, he needs information that explains the causes of actual performance.

RESISTANCE TO CONTROL PROCEDURES

Most managers will resent control devices that they interpret as limiting their freedom to manage, or they may regard the devices as threats to their ability to perform. For this reason, the design of control devices and their use requires that the planner give careful consideration to potential behavioral problems.

Whenever performance standards are introduced resistance to a manpower plan may be aroused. An objective of reducing the attrition rate among recent college hires will require new behavior by managers, which adds to their existing responsibilities. If the objective is unfairly imposed because of unique conditions in some departments, it may be fought with considerable vigor or ignored entirely unless higher management is committed to it.

The organizational awareness of deviation from standards is another sensitive area in control procedures. The exception principle of management operates in control situations. Only non-acceptable performance requires corrective action, and thus poor performance is highlighted. Unfortunately, good performance frequently goes unrecognized.

Control systems may also give rise to behavior that produces satisfactory results in the monitor and analysis stages but which is basically not compatible with the long-run objectives of the manpower plan. As one manager said, "The success of our managers in staying within their manpower budget only proves we have somehow taught our managers to track budget curves. We haven't taught them a thing about good manpower utilization. We are probably overstaffed by fifty per cent in our engineering workforce right now." Another planner said, "We quit forecasting manpower after our first effort because every department head thought he had a carte blanche to hire to the maximum of his department staffing authorization. We stayed within our forecast but the forecast was too high."

Because he may not be able to establish the ideal performance criteria to accompany his manpower plans, the planner must be wary of the trap the standard he does set may create. It may be necessary in some activities to gain experience with a program before establishing control over it. To observe how managers react to new systems aids in designing the control procedures and in redesigning the system itself.

The subjects of perception, attitudes, and motivation have

direct impact on the entire control and evaluation phase. Participation of organizational units in setting objectives and designing action programs helps to overcome these problems. Commitment to the goals of the manpower program is the basic ingredient for success of the program and its control elements. Unit coordinators and other managers may also be involved in designing control systems. When those who will be affected by a control procedure have an opportunity to assist in its design, much of the potential resistance to the procedure may vanish. This participation is especially helpful in eliminating obstrusive and oppressive features of the control system, features often not recognized as such by the system designer but quickly perceived by the persons affected by the system. Finally, communication of the intent of the control activities and how they will be administered is improved through participation. It may not be possible to overcome all forms of resistance, but unless the planner anticipates potential behavioral problems, he may encounter more than he needs to encounter.

CONCLUSION

Goals and objectives against which to measure and evaluate performance are essential to all plans. Program results are analyzed to determine need for corrective action to achieve objectives when performance is not equal to standards set for performance. This action may involve changing either goals or behavior. To change behavior the planner may resort to authority and influence systems, or he may take a longer-run approach and try to improve the quality of his firm's personnel through training and development work.

The control system should service the plan and be acceptable to the organization. The system does not exist for its own sake. As features of it become obsolete, they must be changed. Too frequently control devices are maintained long after the need for them has expired.

The sophistication and cost of control procedures will vary with the importance of the data generated. In some activities relatively simple and inexpensive devices will suffice. In other activities, such as planning for future top management manpower, considerable time and effort may be inexpensive in relation to the usefulness of the information gained.

Behavioral problems in control may cause a good manpower plan to fail. They may also cause managers to shift attention to the activity under control and away from a more important activity. The influence of the manpower manager is affected by the behavioral problems that arise. One test of his influence is his ability to cope with those problems.

That performance standards that service the plan and the control system adequately may be difficult to set is not a sufficient reason to avoid setting standards. Good control is required to achieve objectives and improve long-run plans.

CHAPTER 9

THE ROLE OF THE MANPOWER PLANNER

If you make mistakes in staffing you waste the cost of the time spent in the operation; you waste the time spent in ineffectual attempts to train the wrong recruit; you waste the investment you made in him; you waste a fair proportion of the time of the people working around him — you waste the money spent on getting rid of him — and you risk upheaval among other staff who were perfectly happy until he arrived.

— ERIC WEBSTER

Manpower planning is not a revolutionary new approach to manpower management, nor does it act as a miracle potion to cure all manpower problems. It is, rather, a systematic approach that directs attention to the future and to the identification of potential manpower problems.

It may involve a number of new activities for the planner, most of which involve gathering and analyzing new information. The results are stated as objectives and standards of performance to guide the management of manpower resources. These activities of the manpower planner may project him into the affairs of other managers in an increasingly pronounced manner and thus challenge his behavioral skills.

Manpower planning can be introduced into the organization in several ways. Although in theory a total manpower system might be designed and then introduced, the high cost and failure potential of this method render it impractical for most organizations. Another way is to adopt a greater professional attitude towards all existing activities and upgrade them gradually through planning. Perhaps the most satisfactory introductory method is to identify a few manpower activities that will benefit quickly and visibly from a planning approach.

For many organizations, a thorough inventory of current manpower resources serves as a starting point in a manpower planning program. Such an inventory usually discloses weaknesses in the manpower structure in terms of impending retirements and available replacements. It provides an excellent signal to top management that planning and action are required to overcome the problems revealed by the inventory. The activity undertaken to meet such a situation provides the foundation for further manpower planning work.

An objective, therefore, in initial manpower planning efforts is to identify problems of a magnitude which will impress top management of the need for planning. When the plans are implemented and help to relieve the situation, additional top management support should be forthcoming. The activity will also help convince managers throughout the organization that manpower planning activities benefit them. This accomplishment will help to further convince top managers to lend continued and added support for the manpower planning and programming work.

This philosophy means that some important activities that have a relatively high probability of failure are not undertaken initially. The need to demonstrate capability in manpower planning is more important in the early stages than to attempt the immediate solution of the most difficult manpower problems.

The importance of obtaining top management's support cannot be overemphasized. The activity must function in a "first-class" manner. This does not mean it receives unlimited resources; it does mean, however, that top management gives careful consideration to the findings and recommendations of the planning effort. And it means that other departments provide their support when necessary.

OVERCOMING RESISTANCE TO MANPOWER PLANNING

Opposition to manpower planning, as has been said, may arise from managers throughout the organization. Manpower forecasts that appear as new limitations on hiring authority may create resistance, as may programs that alter manpower mobility and utilization patterns. Attempts to identify the long-range potential of individuals may be scoffed at by managers who have been requested to make the evaluations. Whenever added attention is given to manpower and labor dollars, the planner can expect to find some persons with reasons for opposing any changes.

These behavioral problems may be the most difficult aspect of manpower planning. Developing a good forecasting method challenges his analytical skills, but usually the planner can find solutions to the problems. The challenge of the behavioral problems forces him into human relations situations where the outcome is more uncertain. His ability to tolerate frustration may be severely taxed by these problems.

A host of other kinds of behavioral problems also exist. If the planner is able to gain top management's acceptance of manpower planning and general organizational support for it, he will still encounter a number of special new problems. A program to increase organizational mobility of qualified managers may arouse resentment when he attempts to arrange the transfer of an exceptional manager to another function. If he identifies the need to recruit experienced outside managers, how does he overcome the problems caused by having to pay large salaries to attract these men from their former employers? What kinds of behavioral stress problems is he likely to encounter through a more systematized management of manpower?

These factors require the manpower planner to concentrate a large amount of time on coordination and assistance work. He must work with individual managers who have special manpower problems; he must also attempt to motivate other managers to identify their problems and to "work these problems." Because the manpower resources are influenced directly by managers throughout the organization every day, the manpower planner can not assume that a high quality analysis of the manpower situation will enable the organization to achieve its manpower goals. In one sense, then, the manpower planner should strive to build a "team" attitude towards manpower problems by managers throughout the firm. This attitude is a key link in the success of the manpower planning ventures.

In manpower planning, the work of the behavioral scientists, especially organizational psychologists, is perhaps more important than the work of economists and statisticians. Research on subjects such as perception, motivation, and attitudes provides insights into how to cope with the human relations aspects of manpower planning. In addition, as discussed in Chapter 3, the work of the behavioralists provides guidance for the design of many manpower planning programs.

The results-oriented manager recognizes that his best plans may flounder on the drawingboard because of a lack of behavioral skills. Patience, the ability to relate well with others, good communication skills, and the right amount of agressiveness are essential to success.

A mature political instinct is perhaps the most important quality of the successful manpower manager. Knowing when to be aggressive, where to muster support for a plan, and when to drop a proposal because of lack of support are important. The results-oriented manager knows he cannot always be the nicest or best-liked fellow in the organization. If he feels that he needs to be well liked by everyone, he may not be able to push his programs at strategic times.

LOCATING MANPOWER PLANNING IN THE ORGANIZATION

The amount of organizational support given manpower planning will depend on the quality of the effort. To obtain good support high quality persons must be involved in the activity, and the activity must be high enough in organizational ranking to command attention and gain access to significant company data. Good results will not occur if the manpower planning activity is in an obscure position or is weakly staffed.

The nature of the planning work immediately suggests that the personnel department be responsible for it. This is the location of most manpower planning groups. Sometimes, however, the activity is under the controller or a separate planning group, if personnel fails to plan and others fail to recognize the need for planning.

Locating the activity in the personnel department makes good sense. Personnel already has responsibilities for most of the action program areas, and so should have some ability to perform the work. Further, without the planning responsibility, personnel may not be able to implement plans as intelligently

FIGURE 9-1

POSSIBLE ORGANIZATIONAL DESIGN FOR
MANPOWER PLANNING

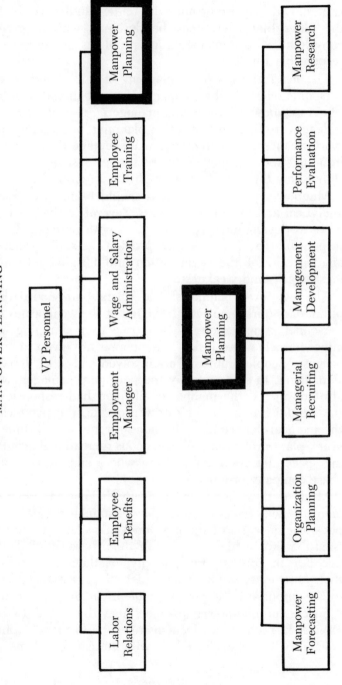

as it should because of not fully understanding them. Finally, the plans themselves may be designed without giving full consideration to implementation problems unless personnel is responsible for them.

The head of manpower planning should report to the top personnel officer in the company. His unit should have specialists in manpower forecasting, managerial recruiting (including college recruiting), organization planning, managerial appraisal (performance and potential), management development and training, and manpower or personnel research. Figure 9-1 shows how the organization might be structured.

Manpower planning positions should be filled by men with analytical and imaginative minds. Several of the positions can serve as development spots for men with potential for higher responsibilities. They can also provide the staff specialist with an overview of the organization and insights into many of its strengths and weaknesses.

The manpower planner should not be burdened with a host of minor and irksome activities. One of the weaknesses of some personnel organizations is their role as a dumping area for minor miscellaneous tasks. These chores are given to personnel because "people problems" are involved and other departments shun them. In one company the personnel manager, who was also considered the manpower planner, had responsibility for the administration of the safety program, the plant cafeteria, the medical department, the house organ, an old-timers' program, plant protection, miscellaneous recreational events, parking space allocation, and a store where employees could purchase company products.

Most of those activities logically belong in other departments. Their assignment to the personnel department dissipates the energies of the personnel manager. In addition, the "snafu" factor is high in many of them because of their sensitive human content. Few, if any, of them lend prestige to their host organization. Their chief effect is reduced attention to the important manpower problems in the organization.

Successful manpower planners may be asked to perform services in these areas. Demonstrated performance ability and an ability to cope effectively with human problems are the planners' identifiable qualifications for the tasks. The temptation may be to assume the duties because the added responsibility and added subordinate manpower may mean a salary increase or increased status. Nevertheless, the long-run consequence of accepting minor detail projects and activities is probably a weaker manpower planning performance, which in turn tends to reduce the opportunity for the manpower planner to demonstrate his qualifications for significant, higher level responsibilities.

CONCLUSION

Manpower planning requires analytical, behavioral, and innovational skills. The challenges to the manpower planner in most organizations are great because of a previous lack of planning attention to many manpower problems.

Because of the lack of information in the manpower literature on analytical techniques in manpower planning, the major thrust of this book has been on presenting methods for the analysis of manpower situations in the organization. This approach emphasizes the need for objectives and goals in manpower management. The author's suggestion that insights into the future are required in setting objectives explains the concern with manpower forecasting and the understanding of its relationship to profit planning.

It is necessary to examine the effects of each manpower activity on other manpower activities. With the aid of a manpower forecast, the planner can establish a wide-coverage, "umbrella" time horizon for manpower objectives. Although this horizon does not eliminate the need for specialized horizons for various programs, it does permit better integration and coordination of programs.

New manpower planning approaches are under development. The action programs described in this book may be quite familiar to planners in some companies. In other companies, serious attention to managerial manpower is only now getting underway.

Few manpower experts, however, would claim knowledge of how to identify the "late bloomers" coming out of college. There are still problems in evaluating the performance and potential of managers, and uncertainty in interpreting all the information gathered in attitude surveys of employees. Only through experimentation, and its accompanying success and failure, does the planner gain insights into vexing problems.

If the manpower planner attempts to approach problems with logic and a spirit of innovation, he will solve some of them. His efforts will lead to further professionalism in manpower management, and his contributions will show up more clearly in the bottom line of the income statement.

GENERAL APPENDIX

MANPOWER FORECASTING LITERATURE

Information on company manpower forecasting methods is frequently sought by manpower planners, but little material is available. In the production, finance, marketing, and general business fields, a considerable amount of forecasting material exists. Many of the forecasting methods used in these areas can be applied to manpower. They are not totally satisfactory, however, because special attention is not given to manpower.

One of the earliest reports on company manpower forecasting describes a procedure used by the Minnesota Mining and Manufacturing Company. At MMM, the ratio of manpower to sales was computed and then applied to sales forecasts to estimate future manpower. The manpower forecasts were used primarily to help determine college recruiting quotas.[1]

A somewhat similar approach was reported for RCA in 1955. A sales-to-employment ratio used to forecast manpower needs was implemented through a management development procedure designed to develop a "second platoon of promotables."[2]

Several articles discuss methods of analyzing the existing managerial workforce to anticipate future manpower problems. Although these efforts do not indicate how to forecast manpower, they show the type of information that an analysis of the current age distribution of managers reveals.[3]

---

[1] Wendel W. Burton, "Forecasting Manpower Needs: A Tested Formula," American Management Association Personnel Series, No. 172, *Practical Methods of Management Development* (New York: American Management Association, 1957), pp. 11-20.

[2] E. Dorsey Foster, "The Role of Economic and Market Research in Long Range Planning," American Management Association Management Report No. 3, *Planning Ahead for Profits* (New York: American Management Association, 1955), p. 45.

[3] See for example John F. Garde, Jr., "The Insidious Management Cycle," *Dun's Review and Modern Industry*, April 1962, p. 54; Bernard Seltzer, "Executive Development: Taking a Management Inventory," *American Business*, February 1953, p. 15; and D. R. Lester and Marjorie L. Owen, "How to Conduct a Manpower Audit," *Personnel*, May-June 1959, pp. 41-51.

Another set of articles discusses the relationship of future manpower requirements to the overall planning effort of the company, and shows the importance of manpower estimates in the overall long-range planning activity.[4]

The military establishment uses statistical analysis of historical staffing ratios to develop staffing guides for military installations. In a personnel office, for example, four clerks might be the suggested manpower to process 1,000 military records and five clerks for 1,500 records. These staffing guides, plus an input-output study of the operation, are used by analysts to develop manpower staffing authorizations for an upcoming period.[5]

In industry comparisons of this type are made by many companies on an exchange basis and by such associations as the American Management Association. By comparing staffing in a function with that of a company similar in type and size, a firm gains some indication of the adequacy of its own staffing. The data frequently do not indicate the differences in activities performed in a function or qualitative differences in manpower, however. In addition, the data do not reveal over- or under-staffing conditions, although information from similar studies can provide important trend data on the manpower growth in organizations.[6]

Researchers at Ohio State University have shown interest in changes in manpower relative to growth of the organization for a considerable time period. Alton W. Baker and Ralph Davis engaged in some early statistical work on the manpower growth of functional units in an organization as related to total employment. By fitting curves to the data they tried to

4 George A. Peck, "The Mechanics of Implementation," *Launching a Company Expansion Program,* Financial Management Series, No. 112 (New York: American Management Association, 1956), pp. 23-24; Guerard H. Howkins, Jr., "Manpower Planning — A Case Study," *N.A.A. Bulletin,* October 1959, p. 65; and Walter S. Wilkstrom, "Factors in Manpower Planning," *Management Record,* September 1960, pp. 2-5.

5 U.S. Department of the Army, Pamphlet No. 20-551, *Staffing Guides for Station Complements* (Washington, D.C.: United States Department of the Army, 1955).

6 For a review of comparative manpower studies in the personnel function see The Conference Board, Studies in Personnel Policy, No. 191 — *Personnel Audits and Reports to Top Management* (New York: National Industrial Conference Board, 1964), pp. 103-105.

show the apparent manpower requirements of staff groups at various total employment levels. Later, Bruce DeSpelder conducted a similar study on the relationship of staff employment growth to total employment growth. Both studies used data gathered at one point in time, and thus do not show the forces that influence manpower requirements over time. The fact that the DeSpelder results differed in several respects from the Baker and Davis results indicates the need for research into the dynamics of manpower staffing over time.[7]

Although primarily of historical significance today, companies engaged in war production in World War II used manning and replacement tables to obtain draft deferments for critical manpower. The tables showed manpower replacement needs for six-month periods and the training period for jobs to be filled. Short-range manpower forecasting and planning was thus widely practiced 25 years ago in American industry.[8]

The accuracy of short-range manpower forecasts is the subject of studies by Robert Ferber at the University of Illinois. Ferber shows a five per cent error in two-month and a seven per cent error in four-month manpower projections furnished state employment security commission offices.[9]

Linear programming is a sophisticated method of determining short-run manpower requirements by examination of several factors of production. Mathematical techniques enable the planner to determine the best economic combination of men and equipment for given output levels. It is assumed that

[7] Alton W. Baker and Ralph C. Davis, *Ratios of Staff to Line Employees and Stages of Differentiation of Staff Functions,* Research Monograph No. 72 (Columbus, Ohio: Bureau of Business Research, Ohio State University, 1954); Bruce DeSpelder, *Ratios of Staff to Line Personnel,* Research Monograph No. 106 (Columbus, Ohio: Bureau of Business Research, Ohio State University, 1962). See also Mason Haire, "Biological Models and Empirical Histories of the Growth of Organizations" for an examination of the dynamics of organization growth in Mason Haire, *Modern Organization Theory* (New York: John Wiley & Sons, 1959), pp. 272-306.

[8] War Manpower Commission documents on these programs are available in some public and university libraries. Directives No. I through V were published in June 1942. Later manning table instructions were published in April and June 1943. See "The Manning Table Plan for Manpower Inventory," *Factory Management and Maintenance,* November 1942, pp. 74-82.

[9] Robert Ferber, *Employers' Forecast of Manpower Requirements: A Case Study* (Urbana, Illinois: Bureau of Economic Research, University of Illinois, 1958).

the men and equipment factors are combined in a linear fashion (i.e., are interchangeable in a straight-line manner in the production process). The influence on manpower of various production volumes, inventory levels, and overtime can be calculated.[10]

Recently a number of researchers have shown interest in studying the flow of manpower through an organization over time with sophisticated mathematical techniques. The armed services have financed a number of these studies because of their large numbers of persons, high attrition rates, and the need to maintain a military capability than can shift significantly in a short time span. These efforts are leading to the formulation of mathematical models for manpower planning.[11]

Another manpower analysis method comes from PERT (Program Evaluation and Review Technique). In PERT manpower skill requirements are estimated and charted to show the demand fluctuations for various skills. The planner strives to level off manpower peaks and valleys to make the best use of his manpower and to avoid excessive layoffs and rehiring. Because PERT is widely used in aerospace work, a major interest with it centers on professional and technical skills.[12]

The United States Navy, which developed PERT, is developing a system to aid in the management of manpower of a complex weapon system. The program, called CAPRI (Computerized Advance Personnel Requirements Information) is designed to help manage the personnel sub-systems of a weap-

---

[10] A large volume of literature exists on this subject. Three references with the least mathematical treatment first are: C. West Churchman, Russell L. Ackoff, and E. Leonard Arnoff, *Introduction to Operations Research* (New York: John Wiley and Sons, Inc., 1957); N. Paul Loomba, *Linear Programming* (New York: McGraw-Hill Book Company, 1964); and George B. Dantzig, *Linear Programming and Extensions* (Princeton, New Jersey: Princeton University Press, 1963).

[11] W. R. Dill, D. P. Gaver, and W. L. Weber, "Models and Modelling for Manpower Planning," *Management Science*, December 1966, pp. B-142 to B-167. This article also contains several references to other mathematical approaches to the subject.

[12] Program Evaluation and Review Technique (PERT) was developed to aid in the development management of the Polaris missile. The Navy estimates that PERT shortened the development time of the Polaris by two years. See United States Department of the Navy, Bureau of Naval Weapons, Special Projects Office, *PERT Summary Report Phase I* (Washington, D.C.: Government Printing Office, 1958).

on system. The network of CAPRI events continues until the last unit of the weapon system is phased out of service and replaced by new weapons. Particularly significant in CAPRI is the development of information to insure that manpower is fully trained and available during the life of a weapon system. In addition, evaluation data on the effectiveness of the manpower plan are generated.[13]

The Human Factors Program of the Navy is an even broader manpower planning program. It is a total systems approach to the manpower management of a weapon system and required support activities. It includes "establishment of a requirement that contractors consider the specific qualifications of Naval personnel when designing systems," and "reorientation of system design to implement trade-offs that will restore the balance between high and low-level skill requirements." This program also encompasses advanced personnel research activity that will help support the weapon system and the entire naval operation.[14]

---

[13] Beck, C. R., et al., The CAPRI System Design and Test Program, Volume 1 — CAPRI System Design and Operation, Operations Research Inc., TR 235, Personnel Research Department of the Navy (Washington, D.C.: United States Department of the Navy, November 1963).

[14] New Developments Research Branch, Bureau of Naval Personnel, New Development Human Factors Program Personnel Research Report No. 64-51 (Washington, D.C.: United States Department of the Navy, 1964), p. IV.

BIBLIOGRAPHY

CHAPTER 1

THE NATURE OF MANAGERIAL MANPOWER PLANNING

Brown, J. Douglas, and Frederick Harbison. *High Talent Manpower for Science and Industry* (Princeton: Princeton University Press, 1957).

Burck, Gilbert. "Knowledge: The Biggest Growth Industry of Them All," *Fortune* (Nov., 1964).

"Educational Obtainments of the Labor Force," *Monthly Labor Review* (March, 1966).

Galbraith, John Kenneth. "Employment, Education and the Industrial System," *Computers and Automation* (Aug., 1965).

Ginzberg, Eli. *Human Resources: The Wealth of a Nation* (New York: Simon & Schuster, 1958).

Goldstein, Harold. "Projections of Manpower Requirements and Supply," *Industrial Relations* (May, 1966).

Hekimian, James S., and Curtis H. Jones. "Put People on Your Balance Sheet," *Harvard Business Review* (Jan.-Feb., 1967).

"Identifying and Developing Managers — World Wide Shortages and Remedies," *The Conference Board Record* (June, 1965).

Kornhauser, William. *Scientists in Industry* (Berkeley: The University of California Press, Bureau of Industrial Relations, 1962).

Lebergott, Stanley. *Manpower in Economic Growth: The United States Record Since 1800* (New York: McGraw-Hill Book Co., 1964).

Lester, Richard A. *Manpower Planning in a Free Society* (Princeton: The Princeton University Press, 1966).

Mangum, Garth L., ed. *The Manpower Revolution* (Garden City, N.Y.: Doubleday & Co., 1965).

Mangum, Garth L., and Arnold L. Nemore. "The Nature and Function of Manpower Projections," *Industrial Relations* (May, 1966).

Marcson, Simon. *The Scientist in American Industry* (New York: Harper and Brothers, 1960).

National Industrial Conference Board. *Population and Economic Growth* (New York: National Industrial Conference Board, Inc., May, 1966).

National Science Foundation. *The Long Range Demand for Scientific and Technical Personnel — A Methodological Study* (Washington, D.C.: U.S. Government Printing Office, 1961).

"Need for Skilled Workers in 1975," *Monthly Labor Review* (April, 1966).

Patton, Arch. "The Coming Scramble for Executive Talent," *Harvard Business Review* (May-June, 1967).

Rosenthal, Neal. "Projections of Manpower Supply in a Specific Occupation," *Monthly Labor Review* (Nov., 1966).

Schultz, Theodore W. "Investment in Human Capital," *American Economic Review* (March, 1961).

Silberman, Charles E. "The Comeback of the Blue-Collar Worker," *Fortune* (Feb., 1965).

Silberman, Charles E. "The Real News About Automation," *Fortune* (Jan., 1965).

"The Growth and Structure of the Labor Force — Projections to 1975," *The Conference Board Record* (Oct., 1965).

U.S. Department of Labor. *Manpower Report of the President and A Report on Manpower Requirements, Resources, Utilization, and Training* (Washington, D.C.: U.S. Government Printing Office, March, 1963; March, 1964; March, 1965; March, 1966; and April, 1967).

Viot, Van H. "The Corporation and Title VII," *The Conference Board Record* (April, 1966).

"What the Civil Rights Act Means to Your Company," *Management Review* (Jan., 1966).

Wishart, Paul B. "Wanted: 200,000 Top Business Managers," *Management Review* (March, 1965).

CHAPTER 2

THE MANPOWER PLANNING PROCESS

American Management Association. *Long-Range Planning in an Expanding Economy,* AMA General Management Series No. 179 (New York: American Management Association, Inc., 1958).

American Management Association. *Planning Ahead for Growth,* AMA General Management Series No. 185 (New York: American Management Association, Inc., 1958).

American Management Association. *Planning Ahead for Profits,* AMA Management Report No. 3 (New York: American Management Association, Inc., 1958).

Anthony, Robert N. *Planning and Control Systems: A Framework for Analysis* (Cambridge: Harvard Business School, Division of Research, 1965).

Branch, Melville C. *The Corporate Planning Process* (New York: American Management Association, Inc., 1962).

Cassell, Frank H. "Manpower Planning: The Basic Policies," *Personnel* (Nov.-Dec., 1965).

Cassidy, Robert F. "Manpower Planning: A Coordinated Approach," *Personnel* (Sept.-Oct., 1963).

Ewing, David W., ed. *Long Range Planning for Management* (New York: Harper & Brothers, Inc., 1958).

Friedman, Jack J. "Long Range Planning and Cloudy Horizons," *Dun's Review and Modern Industry* (Jan., 1963).

Granger, Charles H. "The Hierarchy of Objectives," *Harvard Business Review* (May-June, 1964).

Hardenbrook, Donald J. "Top Management's Use of Long-Range Planning," in *Top Management Handbook,* H. B. Maynard, ed., (New York: McGraw-Hill Book Co., Inc., 1960).

Hardt, Erich. "Manpower Planning," *Personnel Journal* (March, 1967).

Hinrichs, John R. *High Talent Manpower* (New York: American Management Association, Inc., 1966).

LeBreton, Preston P., and Dale A. Henning. *Planning Theory* (Englewood Cliffs, N.J.: Prentice-Hall, Inc., 1961).

Mace, Myles L. "The President and Corporate Planning," *Harvard Business Review* (Jan.-Feb., 1965).

McBeath, Gordon. *Organization and Manpower Planning* (London: Business Publications Limited, 1966).

Platt, William J., and N. Robert Maines. "Pretest Your Long-Range Plans," *Harvard Business Review* (Jan.-Feb., 1959).

Pryblski, Lawrence. "Manpower Planning: Guides Take Out The Guesswork," *Personnel* (Jan.-Feb., 1963).

Ross, Ronald J. "For LRP — Rotating Planners and Doers," *Harvard Business Review* (Jan.-Feb., 1962).

Royce, William S. "Research as a Tool in Long-Range Company Planning," *The Controller* (Nov., 1958).

Scott, Brian W. *Long-Range Planning in American Industry* (New York: American Management Association, Inc., 1965).

Steiner, George A. *Managerial Long-Range Planning* (New York: McGraw-Hill Book Co., Inc. 1963).

"The Status of Long Range Planning," *The Conference Board Record* (Sept., 1966).

Tilles, Seymour. "How to Evaluate Corporate Strategy," *Harvard Business Review* (July-Aug., 1963).

Warren, E. Kirby, *Long Range Planning: The Executive Viewpoint* (Englewood Cliffs, N.J.: Prentice-Hall, Inc., 1966).

CHAPTER 3

MANPOWER PLANNING ACTION PROGRAMS

THE EMPLOYMENT PROCESS

Recruitment — Selection — Placement

Beak, J. R. "Where College Recruiting Goes Wrong," *Personnel* (Sept.-Oct., 1966).

Binlse, Maurice O. "The Clinical Method of Managerial Selection," *Business Horizons* (Spring, 1965).

Bivens, K. K., James Green and G. C. Thompson. "Identifying and Developing Managers — World-Wide Shortages and Remedies," *The Conference Board Record* (June, 1965).

Boyd, J. B. "Interests of Engineers Related to Turnover, Selection, and Management," *Journal of Applied Psychology* (June, 1961).

Dill, William R., Thomas L. Hilton and Walter R. Reitman. *The New Managers* (Englewood Cliffs, N.J.: Prentice-Hall, Inc., 1962).

French, Wendell L. "Psychological Testing: Some Problems and Solutions," *Personnel Administration* (March-April, 1966).

Gellerman, Saul W. "The Ethics of Personality Testing," *Personnel* (Nov.-Dec., 1958).

Ghiselli, Edwin E. "Managerial Talent," *American Psychologist* (Oct., 1963).

Ghiselli, Edwin E. "The Validity of a Personnel Interview," *Personnel Psychology* (Winter, 1966).

Kappel, Frederich R. "From the World of College to the World of Work," *Bell Telephone Magazine* (Spring, 1962).

Lipsett, Laurence, Frank P. Rodgers and Harold M. Kentner. *Personnel Selection and Recruitment* (Boston: Allyn and Bacon, Inc., 1964).

Maloney, P. W. *Management's Talent Search: Recruiting Professional Personnel* (New York: American Management Association, 1961).

Mandell, Milton M. *The Employment Interview* (New York: American Management Association, Inc., 1961).

Mandell, Milton M. *The Selection Process* (New York: American Management Association, Inc., 1964).

Nash, Allan N. "Development of an SVIB Key for Selecting Managers," *Journal of Applied Psychology* (June, 1966).

National Industrial Conference Board. *Employment of the College Graduate*, NICB Studies in Personnel Policy No. 152 (New York: National Industrial Conference Board, 1956).

Odiorne, George S., and Arthur Hann. *Effective College Recruiting* (Ann Arbor: Bureau of Industrial Relations, University of Michigan, 1961).

Odiorne, George S., and Edwin L. Miller. "Selection by Objectives — A New Approach to Managerial Selection," *Management of Personnel Quarterly* (Fall, 1966).

Sands, Edith. *How to Select Executive Personnel* (New York: Reinhold Publishing Corp., 1963).

Schein, Edgar H. "How to Break in the College Graduate," *Harvard Business Review* (Nov.-Dec., 1964).

Souerwine, Andrew H. "More Value from Personnel Testing," *Harvard Business Review* (March-April, 1961).

Stambler, Irwin. "Recruiting Scientists and Engineers," *Industrial Research* (March, 1967).

Strauss, George. "Organization Man — Prospect for the Future," *California Management Review* (Spring, 1964).

Utilization — Promotion — Retirement

American Management Association. *Optimum Use of Engineering Talent* (New York: American Management Association, Inc., 1961).

Berenson, Conrad, and Henry O. Ruhnke. "Job Descriptions: Guidelines for Personnel Management," *Personnel Journal* (Jan., 1966).

Best, Robert D. "What Engineers Want," *Chemical Engineering Progress* (May, 1966).

Bickmore, Lee S. "The Problem of Executive Dropout," *Dun's Review and Modern Industry* (April, 1966).

Bird, Frank. "The Displaced Executive," *Business Topics* (Summer, 1966).

Blood, Jerome W., ed. *The Management of Scientific Talent* (New York: American Management Association, Inc., 1963).

Couch, Peter D., and Earl F. Lundgren. "Making Voluntary Retirement Programs Work," *Personnel Journal* (March, 1963).

Danielson, Lee W. *Characteristics of Engineers and Scientists* (Ann Arbor: Bureau of Industrial Relations, University of Michigan, 1960).

Dinsmore, William. "The Case For Evaluating Professional Jobs," *Personnel* (Nov.-Dec., 1964).

Evans, Gordon H. *Managerial Job Descriptions in Manufacturing* (New York: American Management Association, Inc., 1964).

Faltermayer, Edmund K. "The Drift to Early Retirement," *Fortune* (May, 1965).

Fiedler, Fred E. "Engineer the Job to Fit the Manager," *Harvard Business Review* (Nov.-Dec., 1965).

Garde, John F. "The Insidious Management Cycle," *Dun's Review and Modern Industry* (Dec., 1962).

Gittley, Harvey. "Executive Mobility — The Line/Staff Impasse," *Management Review* (Sept., 1966).

Hamelman, Paul. "Career Development Patterns of Plant Managers," *Industrial Management Review* (Fall, 1966).

Harrell, Thomas W. *Manager's Performance and Personality* (Cincinnati: South-Western Publishing Co., 1961).

Henry, Kenneth. "Top Management Looks at Executive Age and Retirement," *Dun's Review and Modern Industry* (Sept., 1958).

Hulin, Charles L. "The Measurement of Executive Success," *Journal of Applied Psychology* (Oct., 1962).

Johnson, Richard A., and Walter A. Hill. "Management's Dilemma — The Professional Employee," *California Management Review* (Spring, 1963).

Keithley, E. M. "The Office Executive," *California Management Review* (Fall, 1964).

Mayeske, G., and A. Glickman. "Incorporating Retirement Loss Estimates in the Personnel Planning Process," *Public Personnel Review* (Jan., 1967).

Powell, Reed M. "Elements of Executive Promotion," *California Management Review* (Winter, 1963).

Randall, Clarence B. "The Myth of Retirement," *Dun's Review and Modern Industry* (Dec., 1960).

Rhode, Jack F. "Fixed or Variable Retirement Ages," *Personnel Administration* (Jan.-Feb., 1961).

Steward, Nathaniel. "Free the Man Who's Boxed In," *Nation's Business* (July, 1964).

Svenson, Arthur L. "An Augean Stable—The Case of Management Featherbeds," *California Management Review* (Summer, 1963).

Varela, Jacobo A. "Why Promotions Cause Trouble — And How to Avoid It," *Personnel* (Nov.-Dec., 1964).

Webber, Ross A. "What About Promotional Opportunities," *Personnel* (July-Aug., 1962).

DIRECT SUPPORT PROGRAMS

Compensation

Bowen, William. "Executive Compensation: The 'New Wave,'" *Fortune* (Nov., 1964).

Carvalho, Gerald F. "Managing a Dynamic Compensation System," *Management of Personnel Quarterly* (Winter, 1965).

Colvin, C. O. "A Mathematical Exercise in Salaried Personnel Evaluation Theory," *Personnel Journal* (June, 1965).

Diffenbach, William S. "Designing Professional Compensation Plans," *Personnel Journal* (July-Aug., 1964).

Ewing, David W., and Dan H. Fenn, Jr. *Incentives for Executives* (New York: McGraw-Hill Book Co., Inc., 1962).

Foote, George H. "Executive Compensation and the Career Cycle," *Business Horizons* (Spring, 1965).

Foote, George H. "When Deferred Compensation Doesn't Pay," *Harvard Business Review* (May-June, 1964).

Jaques, Elliott. *Equitable Payments* (New York: John Wiley & Co., 1961).

Lawler, Edward E. "The Mythology of Management Compensation," *California Management Review* (Fall, 1966).

Lipstreu, Otis, and W. J. D. Kennedy. "Pricing the Management Job," *Personnel* (Jan.-Feb., 1967).

Otis, Jay L. "A Psychologist Looks at Salary Administration," *Management of Personnel Quarterly* (Summer, 1963).

Patton, Arch. *Men, Money and Motivation* (New York: McGraw-Hill Book Co., Inc., 1961).

Payne, Chester C. "Middle Management Pay for Performance," *The Conference Board Record* (Sept., 1966).

Riegel, John W. *Administration of Salaries and Intangible Rewards for Engineers and Scientists* (Ann Arbor: Bureau of Industrial Relations,

University of Michigan, 1958).

Smyth, Richard C. *Financial Incentives for Executives* (New York: McGraw-Hill Book Co., Inc., 1960).

Torrence, George W. "Maturity Curves and Salary Administration," *Management Record* (Jan., 1962).

"What Executives Think About Pay Levels, Pay Progress, Pay Policies," *Business Management* (Jan., 1967).

Training and Development

American Management Association. *Practical Methods of Management Development*, AMA Personnel Series No. 172 (New York: American Management Association, Inc., 1957).

Blake, R. R., J. S. Mouton, L. B. Barnes and L. E. Greiner. "Breakthrough in Organization Development," *Harvard Business Review* (Nov.-Dec., 1964).

Boehm, George A. W. "Bringing Engineers Up to Date," *Fortune* (May, 1963).

Crissy, William, R. M. Kaplan and L. H. Grossman, "Matrix Model for Planning Executive Development," *Business Topics* (Spring, 1965).

Dill, William, W. B. S. Crowston and E. J. Elton. "Strategies for Self-Education," *Harvard Business Review* (Nov.-Dec., 1965).

Doty, Jack H. "Human Capital Budgeting: Maximizing Returns on Training Investment," *The Journal of Industrial Engineering* (March-April, 1965).

Gitzendanner, Charles. "A Scheme to Involve Managers in Training," *Management of Personnel Quarterly* (Fall, 1966).

Gruenfeld, L. W. "Effects of Fiction Payment and Involvement on Benefits from a Management Development Program," *Journal of Applied Psychology* (Oct., 1966).

Hose, Edgar. "Putting on a Management Development Program that Works," *California Management Review* (Winter, 1966).

House, Robert J. "A Commitment Approach to Management Development," *California Management Review* (Spring, 1965).

Houston, George D. *Manager Development: Principles and Perspectives* (Homewood, Ill.: Richard D. Irwin, Inc., 1961).

Jones, Sidney L. "Meeting the Development Needs of R&D Personnel," *Personnel* (Nov.-Dec., 1962).

Levinson, Harry. "A Psychologist Looks at Executive Development," *Harvard Business Review* (Sept.-Oct., 1962).

Levinson, Harry. "Who Is to Blame for Maladaptive Managers?" *Harvard Business Review* (Nov.-Dec., 1965).

Miner, John B. *The Management of Ineffective Performance* (New York: McGraw-Hill Book Co., Inc., 1963).

National Industrial Conference Board. *College Graduates Assess Their Company Training*, NICB Studies in Personnel Policy No. 188 (New York: National Industrial Conference Board, Inc., 1963).

O'Donovan, Thomas R. "The Climate Approach to Management Development," *Management of Personnel Quarterly* (Summer, 1964).

Raia, Anthony. "A Study of the Educational Value of Management Games," *The Journal of Business* (July, 1966).

Roethlisberger, Fritz J. "Twenty Years of Management Development," *Training Directors Journal* (Sept., 1963).

Stolz, Robert K. "Executive Development — New Perspective," *Harvard Business Review* (May-June, 1966).

Taylor, Jack W. *How to Select and Develop Leaders* (New York: McGraw-Hill

Book Co., Inc., 1962).

Tosi, Henry L. "Management Development and Management by Objectives — An Interrelationship," *Management of Personnel Quarterly* (Summer, 1965).

Tosi, Henry L., and Robert J. House. "Continuing Management Development Beyond the Classroom," *Business Horizons* (Summer, 1966).

Wilkerson, C. David. "A Results-Oriented Development Plan," *The Conference Board Record* (March, 1966).

Wilkstrom, Walter S. *Developing Managerial Competence: Changing Concepts and Emerging Practices* (New York: National Industrial Conference Board, Inc., 1964).

Organization Planning

Alberts, William W., and Jack E. Segall. *The Corporate Merger* (Chicago: The University of Chicago Press, 1966).

Ansoff, H. Igor. "The Firm of the Future," *Harvard Business Review* (Sept.-Oct., 1965).

Ansoff, H. Igor, and J. Fred Weston. "Merger Objectives and Organization Structure," *Quarterly Review of Business and Economics* (Aug., 1962).

Brown, David S. "Shaping the Organization to Fit People," *Management of Personnel Quarterly* (Summer, 1966).

Cerami, Charles A. "You Can Cure Overlapping Management," *Nation's Business* (Oct., 1962).

Dale, Ernest. *Planning and Developing the Company Organization Structure,* AMA Research Report No. 20 (New York: American Management Association, Inc., 1958).

Daniel, Ronald. "Reorganizing for Results," *Harvard Business Review* (Nov.-Dec., 1966).

Fisch, Gerald G. "Stretching the Span of Management," *Harvard Business Review* (Sept.-Oct., 1963).

Forrester, Jay W. "A New Corporate Design," *Industrial Management Review* (Fall, 1965).

Jaques, Elliott. "Too Many Management Levels," *California Management Review* (Fall, 1965).

Klasson, C. R., and K. W. Olm. "Managerial Implications of Integrated Business Operations," *California Management Review* (Fall, 1965).

LeCompte, Kilburn. "Organizational Structures in Transitions," in *Organization Theory in Industrial Practice,* Mason Haire, ed. (New York: John Wiley & Sons, Inc., 1962).

Lorsch, Jay W., and Paul R. Lawrence. "Organizing for Product Innovation," *Harvard Business Review* (Jan.-Feb., 1965).

Mace, Myles L., and George C. Montgomery. *Management Problems of Corporate Acquisitions* (Boston: Harvard University Graduate School of Business Administration, 1962).

Middleton, C. J. "How to Set Up a Project Organization," *Harvard Business Review* (March-April, 1967).

Murray, Thomas J. "Tomorrow — New Configurations for Corporate Structures," *Dun's Review* (Feb., 1967).

Myers, Charles A., ed. *The Impact of Computers on Management* (Boston: the MIT Press, 1967).

National Industrial Conference Board. *Corporate Organization Structures,* NICB Studies in Personnel Policy No. 183 (New York: National Industrial Conference Board, Inc., 1961).

National Industrial Conference Board. *Organization of Staff Functions,* NICB Studies in Personnel Policy No. 165 (New York: National Industrial Conference Board, Inc., 1958).

Schultz, George P., and Thomas L. Whisler. *Management Organization and the Computer* (Glencoe, Ill.: The Free Press of Glencoe, 1960).

Sebring, Thomas H. "Planning for a Personnel Reduction," *Personnel Journal* (April, 1965).

Stieglitz, Harold. "Optimizing Span of Control," *Management Record* (Sept., 1962).

Thompson, James D. *Approaches to Organizational Design* (Pittsburgh: University of Pittsburgh Press, 1966).

Thompson, Robert E. "Span of Control — Conceptions and Misconceptions," *Business Horizons* (Summer, 1964).

White, K. K. *Understanding the Company Organization Chart* (New York: American Management Association, Inc., 1963).

MANPOWER INFORMATION PROGRAMS

Appraisal

Booker, Gene S., and Ronald W. Miller. "A Closer Look at Peer Ratings," *Personnel Magazine* (Jan.-Feb., 1966).

Bray, Douglas W. "The Assessment Center Method of Appraising Management Performance," in *The Personnel Job in a Changing World,* Jerome W. Blood, ed. (New York: American Management Association, Inc., 1964).

Coleman, Charles J. "Avoiding the Pitfalls in Results-Oriented Appraisals," *Personnel Magazine* (Nov.-Dec., 1965).

Executive Study Conference. *Management Games in Selection and Development,* Proceedings of The Executive Study Conference, May 5-6, 1964, Tuxedo, N.Y. (Princeton: Educational Testing Service, 1964).

Farson, Richard E. "Praise Reappraised," *Harvard Business Review* (Sept.-Oct., 1963).

Foundation for Research on Human Behavior. *Assessing Managerial Potential* (Ann Arbor: The Foundation for Research on Human Behavior, 1958).

Hulin, Charles L. "The Measurement of Executive Success," *Journal of Applied Psychology* (Oct., 1962).

Kellogg, Marion S. *What to Do About Performance Appraisal* (New York: American Management Association, Inc., 1965).

Kirkpatrick, Donald L. "Performance Review: Measuring Sticks," *Management of Personnel Quarterly* (Winter, 1966).

Laurent, Harry. "Early Identification of Managers," *Management Record* (May, 1962).

Mahoney, Thomas A., T. H. Jerdee and A. N. Nash. "Predicting Managerial Effectiveness," *Personnel Psychology* (Summer, 1960).

Mahoney, Thomas A., T. H. Jerdee and A. N. Nash. *The Identification of Management Potential — A Research Approach to Management Development* (Dubuque: Wm. C. Brown Co., 1961).

Mayfield, Harold. "In Defense of Performance Appraisals," *Harvard Business Review* (March-April, 1960).

McConkey, Dale D. "Judging Managerial Performance: Single vs. Multiple Levels of Responsibility," *Business Horizons* (Fall, 1964).

McGregor, Douglas. "An Uneasy Look at Performance Appraisals," *Harvard Business Review* (May-June, 1957).

Meyer, Herbert H., E. Kay and J. R. P. French, Jr. "Split Roles in Performance Appraisal," *Harvard Business Review* (Jan.-Feb., 1965).

Odiorne, George S. *Management by Objectives* (New York: Pitman Publishing Corp., 1965).

Patton, Arch. "How to Appraise Executive Performance," *Harvard Business Review* (Jan.-Feb., 1960).

Schleh, Edward C. *Management by Results* (McGraw-Hill Book Co., Inc., 1961).

Spitler, M. E., and W. J. McNamara. "A Managerial Selection Study," *Personnel Psychology* (Spring, 1964).

Standard Oil Co. of New Jersey. *Summary Report of the "Early Identification of Management Potential"* (Linden, N.J.: Social Science Research Division, Employees Relations Dept., Standard Oil Company of New Jersey, Aug., 1961).

Wagner, E. A. "Predicting Success for Young Executives from Objectives Test Scores and Personal Data,'" *Personnel Psychology* (Summer, 1960).

Whisler, Thomas L., and Shirley F. Harper. *Performance Appraisal: Research and Practice* (New York: Holt, Rinehart and Winston, Inc., 1962).

Data Retrieval and Inventory

American Management Association. *Assuring Adequate Reserves of Key Personnel*, AMA Personnel Series No. 169 (New York: American Management Association, Inc., 1957).

American Management Association. *Executive Selection, Development and Inventory*, AMA Personnel Series No. 171 (New York: American Management Association, Inc., 1957).

Austin, Barrie. "The Role of EDP in Personnel," *Management of Personnel Quarterly* (Winter, 1965).

Benge, E. J. "Inventory Your Key Man Talents," *Personnel Journal* (Jan., 1964).

Bronstein, Richard J. "Setting up Skills Inventory: How to Do it on a Shoestring," *Personnel* (March-April, 1965).

Bueschel, Richard. *EDP and Personnel* (New York: American Management Association, Inc., 1966).

Bueschel, Richard T. "Real Time Data Processing for Industrial Relations," *Management of Personnel Quarterly* (Spring, 1966).

Dearden, John. "Can Management Information be Automated?" *Harvard Business Review* (March-April, 1964).

Dearden, John. *Computers in Business Management* (Homewood, Ill.: Dow Jones-Irwin, Inc., 1966).

Dearden, John. "How to Organize Information Systems," *Harvard Business Review* (March-April, 1965).

Kaumeyer, Richard A. "Automated Skills Retrieval: One Company's Program," *Personnel* (Jan.-Feb., 1967).

Lanham, Elizabeth. "EDP in the Personnel Department," *Personnel* (March-April, 1967).

Lester, D. H., and Marjorie L. Owen. "How to Conduct a Manpower Audit," *Personnel* (May-June, 1959).

Marting, Elizabeth, ed. *AMA Book of Employment Forms* (New York: American Management Association, Inc., 1967).

Mathews, A. F. "Keeping Tabs on 7,500 Managers," *Personnel* (May-June, 1966).

Morgan, P. L. "Computers Can Help Select Your Personnel," *Administrative Management* (Nov., 1966).

National Industrial Conference Board. *Forms and Records in Personnel Administration*, Studies in Personnel Policy No. 175 (New York: National Industrial Conference Board, Inc., 1960).

"Skills Inventories — Who Can Do What?" *The Conference Board Record* (Feb., 1964).

Warren, E. Kirby. "The Capability Inventory: Its Role in Long-Range Planning," *Management of Personnel Quarterly* (Winter, 1965).

MP Research

Berry, Dean F. *The Politics of Personnel Research* (Ann Arbor: Bureau of Industrial Relations, University of Michigan, 1967).

Dunnett, Marvin D., and Bernard M. Bass. "Behavioral Scientists and Personnel Management," *Industrial Relations* (May, 1963).

England, George W. "Organizational Goals and Expected Behavior of American Managers," *Academy of Management Journal* (June, 1967).

Ferguson, Laurence L. "How Social Science Research Can Help Management," *California Management Review* (Summer, 1966).

Goode, Cecil E. *Personnel Research Frontiers* (Chicago: Public Personnel Association, 1958).

Laitin, Yale. "Human Relations Research — A Key to Productivity," *Management of Personnel Quarterly* (Spring, 1964).

Lundberg, Craig C. "New Directions for Personnel Research," *Personnel Journal* (Nov., 1962).

Neustadter, Abraham, ed. "What Are the New Frontiers in Research for Personnel Administration?" *Personnel Administration* (July-Aug., 1962).

Patten, Thomas H. "Personnel Research: Status Key," *Management of Personnel Quarterly* (Fall, 1965).

Sayre, Wallace S., and Frederich C. Mosher. *An Agenda for Research in Public Personnel Administration* (Washington, D.C.: National Planning Council, 1959).

Taguiri, Renato, ed. *Research Needs in Executive Selection* (Boston: Harvard University Graduate School of Business Administration, 1961).

"The Role of Research in Industrial Relations/Personnel," *Industrial Relations News Special Report* (July, 1962).

Wortman, Max S. "Corporate Industrial Relations Research—Dream or Reality," *Academy of Management Journal* (June, 1966).

CHAPTER 4

ANALYZING MANAGERIAL MANPOWER REQUIREMENTS

"A Hard Look at Middle Management," *Dun's Review and Modern Industry* (March, 1964).

Alfred, Theodore M. "Checkers or Choice in Manpower Management," *Harvard Business Review* (Jan.-Feb., 1967).

Bursk, Edward C. *The Management Team* (Cambridge: Harvard University Press, 1958).

Caplow, Theodore. "Organization Size," *Administrative Science Quarterly* (March, 1957).

Caskey, Clark C. "Is There a Mess in Middle Management?" *Management of Personnel Quarterly* (Fall, 1964).

Dill, William R., D. P. Gaver and W. L. Weber. "Models and Modelling for Manpower Planning," *Management Science*, Series B. (Dec., 1966).

Ferguson, Lawrence L. "Better Management of Managers' Careers," *Harvard Business Review* (March-April, 1966).

Filley, Alan C. "Decisions and Research in Staff Utilization," *Academy of Management Journal* (Sept., 1963).

Indik, Bernard P. "The Relationship Between Organization Size and Supervision Ratio," *Administrative Science Quarterly* (Dec., 1964).

"Middle Management and Technological Change," *Management Review* (Oct., 1963).

"Middle Managers vs. the Computer," *Dun's Review and Modern Industry* (Nov., 1966).

Monroe, W. H. "Strategy in the Management of Executives," *Business Horizons* (Spring, 1963).

Potter, Curtis J. "The Care and Feeding of Middle Managers," *Management of Personnel Quarterly* (Spring, 1965).

Read, William H. "The Decline of Hierarchy in Industrial Organizations," *Business Horizons* (Fall, 1965).

Schwitter, Joseph. "Computer Effect Upon Managerial Jobs," *Academy of Management Journal* (Sept., 1965).

Shaul, Donald R. "What's Really Ahead for Middle Management?" *Personnel* (Nov.-Dec., 1964).

Starbuck, William. "Organizational Growth and Development," in *Handbook of Organizations,* James March, ed. (New York: Rand McNally, 1965).

Tosi, Henry and Henry Pratt. "Administrative Ratios and Organizational Size," *Academy of Management Journal* (June, 1967).

Uris, Auren. "What's Ahead for Middle Management?" *Chemical Engineering* (Aug., 1963).

CHAPTER 5

THE MEASUREMENT OF LABOR PRODUCTIVITY

Crossman, E. R. F. W. "Automation, Skill and Manpower Predictions," U.S. Department of Labor, Office of Manpower Policy, Evaluation and Research, *Seminar on Manpower Policy and Program* (Washington, D.C.: U.S. Government Printing Office, Sept., 1966).

Davis, Hiram. *Productivity Accounting* (Philadelphia: University of Pennsylvania Press, 1956).

Dressel, R. L. "Input-Output Relationships as a Forecasting Tool," *NAA Bulletin* (June, 1962).

Dunlop, John T., and V. P. Diatchenko, eds. *Labor Productivity* (New York: McGraw-Hill Book Co., Inc., 1964).

Ernst, Harry. "Accounting for Productivity Changes," *Harvard Business Review* (May-June, 1956).

European Productivity Agency. *Productivity Measurement: Concepts* (Paris: Organization for European Economic Cooperation, 1955).

Fabricant, Solomon. *Basic Facts on Productivity Change.* National Bureau of Economic Research Occasional Paper No. 63 (Princeton: Princeton University Press, 1959).

Fabricant, Solomon. "Meaning and Measurement of Productivity" in *Labor Productivity,* John T. Dunlop and V. P. Diatchenko, eds. (New York: McGraw-Hill Book Co., 1964).

Fabricant, Solomon. "Measurement of Technological Change," U.S. Department of Labor, Office of Manpower Policy, Evaluation and Research, *Seminar on*

Manpower Policy and Program (Washington, D.C.: U.S. Government Printing Office, July, 1965).

Frankel, Marvin. "The Production Function in Allocation and Growth: A Synthesis,"*American Economic Review* (Dec., 1962).

Gold, Bela. *Foundations of Productivity Analysis* (Pittsburgh: University of Pittsburgh Press, 1955).

Hardin, Elinar. "Measuring the Rate of Productivity Growth," *Productivity Measurement Review* (Nov., 1963).

Kendrick, John W., and Daniel Creamer. *Measuring Company Productivity*, National Industrial Conference Board Studies in Business Economics No. 74 (New York: National Industrial Conference Board, Inc., 1961).

Martin, Harold W. "Productivity Measurement and Control," *Productivity Measurement Review* (May, 1960).

Most, Kenneth S. "Practical Problems in Measuring Productivity," *The Accountant* (Dec. 7, 1963).

Myers, Charles A., ed. *Wages, Prices, Profits, and Productivity* (New York: Columbia University Press, 1959).

National Bureau of Economic Research. *Output, Input, and Productivity Measurement*, National Bureau of Economic Research Studies in Income and Wealth, Vol. 25 (Princeton: Princeton University Press, 1961).

Pesek, B. P. "Economic Growth and Its Measurement," *Economic Development and Cultural Change* (April, 1961).

Rosen, Hjalmar, and Edward F. McCallum. "Correlates of Productivity," *Personnel Psychology* (Winter, 1962).

Smith, Vernon L. *Investment and Production* (Cambridge: Harvard University Press, 1961).

Upgren, Arthur R. *Productivity, Pay and Prices* (St. Paul, Minn.: Macalester College, 1964).

U.S. Bureau of Labor Statistics. *Indexes of Output per Manhour for Selected Industries, 1939 and 1947-60* (Washington, D.C.: U.S. Government Printing Office, 1961).

CHAPTER 6

MAKING A MANPOWER FORECAST

Andress, Frank J. "The Learning Curve as a Production Tool," *Harvard Business Review* (Jan.-Feb., 1954).

Ardner, J. Walter. "Sales Forecasting Methods and Their Place in Long Range Planning," *NAA Bulletin* (Aug., 1958).

Burton, Wendel W. "Forecasting Manpower Needs — A Tested Formula" in *Labor and Management Face the Future*, AMA Personnel Series No. 172 (New York: American Management Association, Inc., 1957).

Butler, William F., and Robert Kavesh. *How Business Economists Forecast* (Englewood Cliffs, N.J.: Prentice-Hall, Inc., 1966).

Controllership Foundation. *Business Forecasting: A Survey of Business Practices and Methods* (New York: Controllership Foundation, Inc., 1950).

DeSpelder, Bruce E. *Ratios of Staff to Line Personnel* (Bureau of Business Research, Ohio State University, 1962).

Dowd, James. "The Controller's Responsibility for Forecasting," *The Controller* (April, 1955).

Ferber, Robert. *Employers' Forecasts of Manpower Requirements: A Case Study* (Urbana, Ill.: Bureau of Economic and Business Research, University of Illinois, 1958).

Foster, E. Dorsey. "The Role of Economic and Market Research in Long Range Planning," in *Planning Ahead for Profits*, AMA Management Report No. 3 (New York: American Management Association, Inc., 1955).

Haire, Mason. "Biological Models and Empirical Histories of the Growth of Organizations," in *Modern Organization Theory*, Mason Haire, ed. (New York: John Wiley & Sons, Inc., 1959).

Hammond, Robert A. "Making OR Effective for Management," *Business Horizons* (Spring, 1962).

Knapp, Robert A. "Forecasting and Measuring with Correlation Analysis," *Financial Executive* (May, 1963).

Levy, Ferdinand K., L. Thompson and J. D. West. "The ABCs of the Critical Path Method," *Harvard Business Review* (Sept.-Oct., 1963).

National Industrial Conference Board. *Forecasting Sales*, Studies in Business Policy No. 106 (New York: National Industrial Conference Board, Inc., 1961).

Peck, George A. "The Mechanics of Implementation," in *Launching a Company Expansion Program*, AMA Financial Management Series No. 112 (New York: Amerian Management Association, Inc., 1956).

Spencer, Milton H., C. G. Clark and P. W. Hoguet. *Business and Economic Forecasts* (Homewood, Ill.: Richard D. Irwin, Inc., 1961).

Vetter, Eric W. "How to Forecast your Manpower Needs," *Nation's Business* (Feb., 1964).

Wilson, Charles Z., and Marcus Alexis. "Basic Frameworks for Decisions," *Journal of the Academy of Management* (Aug., 1962).

Wolfe, Harry D. *Business Forecasting Methods* (New York: Holt, Rinehart and Winston, Inc., 1966).

CHAPTER 7

THE MANPOWER FORECAST AND CORPORATE PROFIT OBJECTIVES

Anthony, Robert N. "Some Fallacies in Figuring Return on Investment," *NAA Bulletin* (Dec., 1960).

Arnstein, William E. "The Fundamentals of Profit Planning," *The New York Certified Public Accountant* (May, 1962).

Backer, Morton. "Additional Considerations in Return on Investment Analysis," *NAA Bulletin* (Jan., 1962).

Davison, E. Hay. "Productivity and the Industrial Accountant," *The Accountant* (Nov. 30, 1963).

Dawes, Irving D. "Profit Planning: The Controller's Part," *The Controller* (April, 1955).

Doofe, Henry C. "The Profit Path as Seen Through the Budgetary Control Program," *NAA Bulletin* (Nov., 1959).

Forrester, Jay W. *Industrial Dynamics* (Cambridge: The MIT Press, 1961).

Gelvin, L. M. "Return on Investment Concept and Corporate Policy," *NAA Bulletin* (July, 1961).

Gordon, Myron J. "The Payoff Period and the Rate of Return," *The Journal of Business* (Oct., 1955).

Hertz, David B. "Risk Analysis in Capital Investment," *Harvard Business Review* (Jan.-Feb., 1964).

Jones, Ralph C. *Price Level Changes and Financial Statements — Case Studies of*

Four Companies (New Haven, Conn.: American Accounting Association, 1955).

Magee, John F. "Decision Trees for Decision Making," *Harvard Business Review* (July-Aug., 1964).

Magee, John F. "How to Use Decision Trees in Capital Investment," *Harvard Business Review* (Sept.-Oct., 1964).

Mattessich, Richard. "Budgeting Models and Systems Simulation," *The Accounting Review* (July, 1961).

McEwan, W. J. R. "Productivity and Profits," *The Accountant* (May 9, 1964).

Moore, Carl C. "The Concept of the P/V Graph Applied to Capital Investment Planning," *The Accounting Review* (Oct., 1962).

Mutton, A. R. "Changes in Money Values from an Accountant's Standpoint," *The Australian Accountant* (Aug., 1962).

National Association of Accountants. *Long Range Profit Planning*, NAA Research Report No. 42 (New York: National Association of Accountants, Dec., 1964.)

Rapaport, Leo A., and William P. Drews. "Mathematical Approach to Long-Range Planning," *Harvard Business Review* (May-June, 1962).

Solomon, Ezra. "Return on Investment: The Relation of Book-Yield to True Yield," in *Research in Accounting Measurement*, Robert Jaedicke, Yuji Ijiri and Oswald Nielsen, eds. Collected Papers of the American Accounting Association (Menasha, Wisc.: American Accounting Association, 1966).

Solomon, Ezra. "The Arithmetic of Capital Budgeting Decisions," *The Journal of Business* (April, 1956).

Vazsonyi, Andrew. "Statistical Techniques for Financial Planning and Forecasting," *The Controller* (May, 1957).

Welsch, Glenn A. *Budgeting: Profit Planning and Control* (Englewood Cliffs, N.J.: Prentice-Hall, Inc., 1960).

Weston, J. Fred. "Financial Implications of Growth," *The Controller* (March, 1958).

Weston, J. Fred. "Forecasting Financial Requirements," *The Accounting Review* (July, 1958).

Wickmann, William C. "The Accountants Contribution to Long Term Planning," *N.A.C.A. Bulletin* (July, 1955).

CHAPTER 8

CONTROL AND EVALUATION

Argyris, Chris. "Human Problems with Budgets," *Harvard Business Review* (Jan.-Feb., 1953).

Ashby, W. Ross. *An Introduction to Cybernetics* (New York: John Wiley and Sons, Inc., 1965).

Beer, Stafford. *Cybernetics and Management* (New York: John Wiley and Sons, Inc., 1964).

Bennis, Warren G., Kenneth D. Benne and Robert Chin, eds. *The Planning of Change* (New York: Holt, Rinehart & Winston, 1961).

Bonini, Charles P., Robert K. Jaedicke and Harvey M. Wagner. *Management Controls* (New York: McGraw-Hill Book Co., 1964).

Boulding, Elise, ed. *Conflict Management in Organizations* (Ann Arbor: Foundation for Research on Human Behavior, 1961).

Dauten, Paul M., Homer L. Gammill and Stanley C. Robinson. "Emerging Concepts of Managerial Control," *Journal of the Academy of Management* (Dec., 1958).

Emch, Arnold F. "Control Means Action," *Harvard Business Review* (Sept.-Oct., 1964).

Ginzberg, Eli, and Ewing W. Reilley. *Effecting Change in Large Organizations* (New York: Columbia University Press, 1957).

Gray, Robert D. "Evaluating the Personnel Department," *Personnel* (March-April, 1965).

House, Robert J. "An Experiment in the Use of Management Training Standards," *Journal of the Academy of Management* (April, 1962).

Lemke, B. C., and James D. Edwards. *Administrative Control and Executive Action* (Columbus, Ohio: Charles E. Merrill Books, Inc., 1961).

Likert, Rensis. "Measuring Organizational Performance," *Harvard Business Review* (March-April, 1958).

Luck, Thomas J. *Personnel Audit and Appraisal* (New York: McGraw-Hill Book Co., Inc., 1955).

Malcolm, D. G., and A. J. Rowe. "An Approach to Computer-based Management Control Systems," *California Management Review* (Spring, 1961).

Mann, Floyd G., and Franklin W. Neff. *Managing Change in Organizations* (Ann Arbor: The Foundation for Research on Human Behavior, 1961).

National Industrial Conference Board. *Personnel Audits and Reports to Top Management*, Studies in Personnel Policy No. 191 (New York: National Industrial Conference Board, Inc., 1964).

Odiorne, George S. "Evaluation of Management Training," *Journal of the American Society of Training Directors* (March, 1961).

"Plotting Future Manpower Requirements," *Management Review* (Dec., 1961).

Rabe, W. F. "Yardsticks for Measuring Personnel Department Effectiveness," *Personnel* (Jan.-Feb., 1967).

Roberts, Edward B. "Industrial Dynamics and the Design of Management Control Systems," *Management Technology* (Dec., 1963).

Scheid, Phil N. "Charter of Accountability for Executives," *Harvard Business Review* (July-Aug., 1965).

Sord, Burnard H., and Glenn A. Welsch. *Business Budgeting: A Survey of Management Planning and Control Practices* (New York: Controllership Foundation, Inc., 1958).

Tomb, John O. "A New Way to Management Integrated Planning and Control," *California Management Review* (Fall, 1962).

Torrence, William D. "Some Personnel Auditing Practices in Business and Industry," *Personnel Journal* (Sept., 1962).

Wikstrom, Walter S. "Charting Management Manpower Plans," *Management Record* (July-Aug., 1961).

CHAPTER 9

THE ROLE OF THE MANPOWER PLANNER

American Management Association. *The Personnel Man and His Job* (New York: American Management Association, Inc., 1962).

Anshen, Melvin, and George Leland Bach. *Management and Corporation, 1985* (New York: McGraw-Hill Book Co., Inc., 1960).

Bailey, J. K., and A. H. Savage. "How Pure Should the Staff Be?" *Personnel Administration* (Sept.-Oct., 1965).

Blood, Jerome W., ed. *The Personnel Job in a Changing World* (New York: American Management Association, Inc., 1964).

Costello, Timothy W., and Sheldon S. Zalkind. *Psychology in Administration* (Englewood Cliffs, N.J.: Prentice-Hall, Inc., 1963).

French, Wendell. *The Personnel Management Process: Human Resources Administration* (Boston: Houghton Mifflin Co., 1964).

Leavitt, Harold J., and Thomas L. Whisler. "Management in the 1980's," *Harvard Business Review* (Nov.-Dec., 1958).

Langer, Allen. "Structuring the Corporation Personnel Staff," *The Conference Board Record* (May, 1965).

Marriner, Harvey F. "Rx for the Personnel Man With Too Many Hats," *Personnel* (March-April, 1961).

McFarland, Dalton F. *Company Officers Assess the Personnel Function*, AMA Research Study No. 79 (New York: American Management Association, Inc., 1967).

McFarland, Dalton F. *Cooperation and Conflict in Personnel Administration* (New York: American Foundation for Management Research, 1962).

National Industrial Conference Board. *Personnel Administration: Changing Scope and Organization*, NICB Studies in Personnel Policy, No. 203 (New York: National Industrial Conference Board, Inc., 1966).

Odiorne, George S. *How Managers Make Things Happen* (New York: Prentice-Hall, Inc., 1961).

Rico, Leonard. "Managerial Schizophrenia: The Personnel Function in a Firm," *Management of Personnel Quarterly* (Winter, 1965).

Simon, Herbert A. *The New Science of Management Decision* (New York: Harper and Brothers, 1960).

Toedt, T. A., et al. *Managing Manpower in the Industrial Environment* (Dubuque: Wm. C. Brown Co., Inc., 1962).

Volante, Elena M. "Are Personnel People Functioning as Tinkerers or Professionals?" *Management of Personnel Quarterly* (Summer, 1965).

Ways, Max. "Tomorrow's Management," *Fortune* (July, 1966).